HARDY HOLZMAN PFEIFFER ASSOCIATES

BUILDINGS AND PROJECTS 1992–1998

FOREWORD BY MILDRED FRIEDMAN
INTRODUCTION BY GLENN M. ANDRES
BUILDING DESCRIPTIONS BY DEBRA WATERS

RIZZOLI
NEW YORK

ACKNOWLEDGMENTS

First published in the United States of America
in 1999 by
Rizzoli International Publications, Inc.
300 Park Avenue South
New York, NY 10010

Copyright © 1999
Rizzoli International Publications, Inc.

"Hardy Holzman Pfeiffer Associates:
On Making Architecture"
© 1999 Glenn M. Andres

ISBN   0-8478-2208-7 (HC)
          0-8478-2217-6 (PB)

LC   99-70711

Designed by Abigail Sturges

Printed and bound in Singapore

HHPA's accomplishments can be largely attributed to our collaborative approach, as effective now as at our founding in 1967, in which project ideas are collectively explored, debated, and developed. The opening of our Los Angeles office, in 1986, and the growing complexity of our projects have gradually widened the collaborative circle beyond the three original partners to include associates, senior associates, and associate partners. We believe the future success of the firm rests with this group, who have the full array of skills—from programming to master planning, design to construction, and computer expertise to project management—to properly serve our clients. While these senior staff members advocate the principles that have guided us over the past three decades, they also look forward to making their own contributions to the profession. We take great pleasure in the opportunity to join forces with this new generation of HHPA leaders.

We are grateful to Rizzoli senior editor David Morton for so carefully watching over the development of this second volume on HHPA, and to Abigail Sturges, the book's graphic designer, who brought her usual unerring eye to the assignment. Thanks also to Glenn Andres for his essay, which eloquently relates our most recent work to our earlier endeavors. And we are delighted to have Mildred Friedman's insightful foreward.

Debbi Waters, HHPA's Director of Marketing, accomplished two herculean tasks. Not only did she write thoughtful, concise accounts of each project, but she also administered the monograph's production from its conception, orchestrating the participation of Heather Byron-Cox, Foaad Farah, Jean Marie Gath, Stephen Johnson, Elizabeth Kubany, Geoff Lynch, and Susan Packard, whose writing, editing, and drawing contributions were invaluable. Special mention must be made of Jessica McCormack's sterling work in assembling and organizing every illustration in the book (and all those that were not included).

We take pride in being able to draw on the nearly four decades of work completed and thank all our staff for their untiring efforts.

FOREWORD
Mildred Friedman

For more than twenty years the firm of Hardy Holzman Pfeiffer Associates has played a significant role in my architectural education. In 1972, because I so admired their innovative design for the Mt. Healthy School, in Columbus, Indiana, I invited the team to develop an exhibition for the Walker Art Center, in Minneapolis. They were asked to create an exhibition dealing with new ways and new places to provide children with positive learning experiences. What they delivered was an amazing collection of ad-hoc environments embodying startling new ideas. Their efforts, which occurred at the very beginning of the current age of electronic technology, demonstrated that they understood the enormous impact it would have on future schools. Their ingenious planning incorporated some of technology's solid inventions with transforming concepts about visual delight and physical comfort—elements that continue to characterize their work. Their 1974 exhibition, *New Learning Spaces & Places*, was a success on many levels: high-school students demonstrated new tools for a fascinated public, challenging accepted systems and indicating new directions for educators and students alike.

The firm is now bicoastal. Hugh Hardy and Malcolm Holzman are in New York, Norman Pfeiffer is in Los Angeles. Schools continue to be an important part of their practice, and three new buildings devoted to the arts are major additions to that history. The Dance Theatre of Harlem's Everett Center provides this unique school and professional dance company with its main studio, classrooms, parents' lounge, and offices. With this handsome new building, HHPA has created a lively complex alongside the converted garage structure that was their modest first home. Vermont's Middlebury College commissioned HHPA to create a center for the arts, to include a museum, a concert hall, a theater, and a dance studio. The building's four primary elements, clad in split-faced gray granite and rough-cut pink granite, are tied together with New England clapboard walls and copper roofing. Used by both the school and the surrounding community, these inviting spaces have brought town and gown together in a remarkable synergy. The firm's Colburn School of Performing Arts, on Los Angeles's Grand Avenue, is a stunning new landmark in the city's expanding downtown cultural district. Its landscaped plaza provides a perfect place for outdoor performances and a direct connection to the neighboring Museum of Contemporary Art.

HHPA is especially renowned for its theater and performing arts complexes. Many are new projects and a number of others are exquisite renovations. Two representative works, in a genre they have termed "interpretive restoration," are on New York's 42nd Street, in the heart of its historic theater district, which is currently experiencing an impressive regeneration. The New Victory and New Amsterdam theaters are exemplary in that their brilliant renewals are respectful of but not overwhelmed by their pasts.

Other historically significant places given new life by HHPA include Bertrand Goodhue's 1926 Los Angeles Central Public Library, beautifully integrated with the firm's new Tom Bradley Wing. Its dramatic eight-story, glass-roofed atrium is filled with commissioned works of art that echo the spirit of those in the Goodhue building. In collaboration with the landscape architect Laurie Olin and the garden designer Lynden Miller, HHPA has brought Bryant Park, behind New York City's Public Library, back to life. This formerly desolate public space has been reborn as a much-needed urban oasis for the working population of midtown Manhattan. Its elegant, vine-covered restaurant includes a rooftop dining area that overlooks the park's wide, welcoming greensward. Similarly, as part of its Cleveland Public Library project, in the heart of downtown, HHPA has redeveloped the Eastman Reading Garden. Undertaken with Olin and the artists Tom Otterness and Maya Lin, it reinvigorates this popular resting place, whose gentility is a perfect counterpart to the modernized Main Library and bold new Louis Stokes Wing.

Their acclaimed 1987 renovation of Rockefeller Center's Rainbow Room will soon be joined there by a new project, one that for HHPA may be its most daunting yet: Radio City Music Hall. To bring back the Hall's splendor, its mad 1930s glitz, while providing new amenities and essential contemporary technologies, is a challenge they will surely respond to with the knowledge and care that have been the firm's hallmarks. At Radio City they are again asked to demonstrate that it is possible for tradition and innovation to coexist in perfect harmony.

In addition to new freestanding buildings and restorations of significant historical structures, HHPA is working on innumerable master-planning projects for arts institutions, libraries, and college campuses. The largest of these, a 103-acre Southern California hilltop campus for Soka University of America, will result in more than 500,000 square feet of construction in its first phase alone. It is conceived of as an academic village, in which carefully sited clusters of buildings and courtyards will foster a dialogue between students and faculty. And in New York, the firm has been involved for more than twenty years in proposals for Bridgemarket, a commercial development to be located in the vaults of Manhattan's Queensboro Bridge. When it is completed, in 1999, HHPA, with its matchless sensibility, will again have revitalized a long-neglected urban landmark.

HHPA's work is distinctive for its aesthetic daring, fresh combinations of materials, patterns, and colors, innovative use of off-the-shelf components, and theatrical élan. And the firm's approach in both its new and renewal projects is always carried out with an assured light touch. As you will see in the following pages, their exuberant work, which captures the spirit of popular culture in our rapidly evolving society, has been combined with a sophistication of expression that defines this vital, mature practice.

CONTENTS

1 Sorkin, M. *Hardy Holzman Pfeiffer,* New York:
Whitney Library of Design, 1981;
*Hardy Holzman Pfeiffer Associates, Buildings and
Projects 1967–1992.* New York: Rizzoli, 1992;
Middlebury College Museum of Art, *Hardy Holzman
Pfeiffer Associates: Concepts and Buildings,*
Middlebury, VT 1993.
2 Diamondstein, B. *American Architecture Now II.*
New York: Rizzoli, 1985, p. 186.

8

1

HARDY HOLZMAN PFEIFFER ASSOCIATES: ON MAKING ARCHITECTURE

Glenn M. Andres

As it embarks upon its fourth decade, Hardy Holzman Pfeiffer Associates is operating in prime time. To date the vital partnership has produced nearly five hundred buildings and planning projects, been the subject of monographs and exhibitions,[1] and won more than one hundred design awards. Creative careers of such length have a tendency to go through cycles — from early, attention-catching, innovative gestures, through heroic mid-career statements, to formulaic self-quotation (a tendency supported, if not virtually demanded, by patrons seeking a continuation of proven images and past successes). The pattern holds true for HHPA, except for the last part, for in each new generation of buildings they continue to impress with the inventiveness of their planning solutions, the urbanity of their public spaces, the surprise of their materials, and the freshness of their sometimes brash decor.

They began, by their own confession, as young designers growing up together and rejecting everything. Part of the first post-modern generation, they reacted against the "less-is-more" solutions of an International Style Modernism that sought supreme, if also rather homogeneous, elegance by excluding many of the messier functional and contextual issues inherent in architecture. Their approach was inclusive. They embraced particularities of function, climate, setting, and theme as invitations to shrug off modernism's ahistorical, orthogonal, pristinely technolgical straitjacket. They declared themselves with a loft office outfitted in a notorious mix of chartreuse beams, old Roxy Theatre carpeting, framed "credentials" (an army discharge, an elementary school diploma), and the neon proclamation "A spicier New York is up to you." They composed with gridshifts, found objects, off-the-shelf details, exposed utilities, and bold colors. They communicated conceptually in a pop shorthand where buildings could be "gift boxes," "watermelons," or "chocolate chip cookies." And they produced iconic designs like the Salisbury, Maryland, Elementary School (1972) — a modest-budget square box with a skewed platform, eccentrically quartered by enclosed diagonal volumes to leave unexpected and characterful residual open-classroom spaces.

3

Soon they were producing higher profile projects for a circle of adventuresome corporate and institutional clients. In Richmond, Virginia, they built the Best Products Headquarters (1978–80) as the collision of an orthogonal office scheme with the segment of a great circle and decked it out in collected and commissioned art and references to medieval and Renaissance Italy, colonial America, and Art Deco New York.

In Los Angeles (1981–86) they created a new master plan for the Los Angeles County Museum of Art, transforming William Pereira's three quiet 1960s pavilions around a pool-turned-plaza by means of a dramatically inserted gallery addition, a lively central lobby/court, and an image-making monumental entrance façade. In Brooklyn (1987) they updated and reconfigured the derelict Majestic Theatre into an evocative but functional ruin for the Brooklyn Academy of Music. A string of such commissions, along with the 1981 AIA Firm Honor Award for their original and varied work, attested to the stature achieved by the erstwhile iconoclasts as, in the words of one critic, the "designated off-the-wall architect[s] of the respectable middle."[2]

Today's HHPA operates from bases on both coasts. They fill expanded quarters behind New York's Flatiron Building on Broadway and a second office (established 1987) in downtown Los Angeles's landmark Fine Arts Building. The neon sign is still a presence, but now the wild carpets are of their own designs and the characterful clutter comprises myriad study models and examples of custom furniture and lighting fixtures from past and current projects. The firm has left its mark on so many major public and cultural projects in so many urban centers (Manhattan to Honolulu, Anchorage to Charlotte) and on so many campuses (Bowdoin to Stanford, Middlebury to Texas Christian) that it has been likened to McKim, Mead, & White. Their commissions include theaters, libraries, concert halls, musuems, academic facilities, corporate offices, houses of worship, restaurants, and civic spaces. They are entrusted with the reworking of beloved cultural artifacts. Their materials are richer. No longer considered so outlandish, many of their design constants have won the endorsement of emulation by colleagues.

9

4. *Orchestra Hall, concert hall*
5. *Orchestra Hall, north façade*
6. *Whitaker Center for Science and the Arts, street level plan*

10

Yet in its successful maturity HHPA has neither lapsed into self-quotation nor lost its power to provoke. The designs in this volume are hardly formulaic replays of past successes. A comparison of the San Angelo Museum, the Colburn School, the Vassar College Library, and the New Amsterdam Theatre makes it evident that there is still no stock HHPA image. This is a firm that has always prided itself on the idea that, generated to serve specific circumstances, no two of its buildings look alike. Trying to generalize about HHPA on the basis of one or another of their projects would be about as accurate as the blind men trying to describe an elephant on the basis of the particular part each was touching. While the recent work bears no immediately identifiable signature aesthetic, however, it is notable for its consistency of approach. It remains solidly based in principles that have informed and unified the firm's production since the beginnings of the partnership. As many of their contemporaries have narrowed postmodernism into so many concrete styles — High-Tech, Classicism, Deconstruction — HHPA has stayed true to it as a versatile set of attitudes toward making architecture.

Fundamental is their abiding sense of design as a collaborative undertaking. In the 1960s this meant the creative melding of the varied but complementary outlooks of Hugh Hardy, Malcolm Holzman, and Norman Pfeiffer. Whichever partner had charge of a project brainstormed with and received the commentary of the others to the point that few of the designs could be assigned to a specific personal outlook among the trio. As the firm has grown and the scope of its commissions has expanded from individual buildings into larger-scale planning projects for parks (Enchanted Skies), campuses (Soka University, the University of Kentucky), and urban districts (Salt Lake City Cultural Plan), its organization has become more complex and its design collaboration far broader. It relies on the increasingly important participation of long-term associates and on in-house collaborative design groups with special expertise in such areas as libraries, theaters, cultural facilities, planning and programming, education, retail/entertainment, historic renovation, and interiors. Yet through the direct participation of one of the founding partners

4

5

6

in every design team and with the aid of today's rapid and sophisticated communication technologies, the dialogue remains a vital part of the firm's operation and assures that each HHPA design is still conditioned by ingrained attitudes and the richly creative and idiosyncratic design process forged in the partnership's early days.

Basic to that process is a programmatic analysis that deconstructs buildings into their components — special functional containers, circulation, mechanicals, organizational systems, entrances, façades — and then treats these as something of a kit of parts out of which to make architecture. Important among these parts, the major spaces of a building become separate design units that can be addressed independently in terms of such criteria as use, scale, acoustics, character, and environment. It is an approach that, since early projects like Minneapolis's Orchestra Hall (1974), has facilitated the creation of a string of memorable rooms. Some, like the sanctuary of Temple Israel and the concert hall at the Colburn School are quite formal. In other cases programmatic concerns can result in less regular spaces, like the studio theaters at Middlebury and Texas Christian University, that purposely defy formal resolution in order to encourage as many patterns of use as there are artistic imaginations. Designed from the inside out and studied by means of independent models, each has been configured more in response to its specific requirements than by the constraints of some ultimate building envelope.

The distinctive, often nonorthogonal, volumes of these parts are permitted to read inside and outside the building in a manner that has been consistent for HHPA design from Minneapolis's Orchestra Hall to the more recent University of North Texas Murchison Performing Arts Center in Denton, Texas. They act as strong elements in the design's visual vocabulary, used in conjunction with other favorite HHPA forms. Notable among the latter are sine curves, used variously in elevation (as at the Highland House) and in plan (as in the "wiggle wall" at the University of Nebraska, Omaha) and the segmental curves and folded walls seen in plans like that of the Whitaker Center. These visually significant components are assembled into

7. Mount Healthy School, plan
8. Scholastic Inc. Headquarters, carpet patterned with company creed
9. Los Angeles County Museum of Art, Anderson Building façade on Wilshire Boulevard
10. Dance Theatre of Harlem, shingles set in diamond pattern

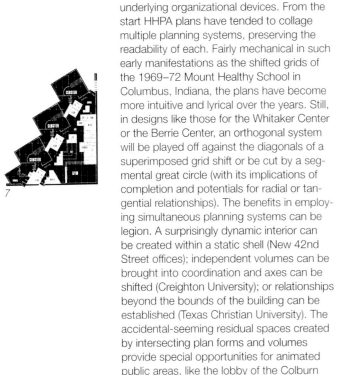

7

a building through a process of juxtaposition that may impart an arbitrary, ad hoc visual quality to the design but is actually ruled by underlying organizational devices. From the start HHPA plans have tended to collage multiple planning systems, preserving the readability of each. Fairly mechanical in such early manifestations as the shifted grids of the 1969–72 Mount Healthy School in Columbus, Indiana, the plans have become more intuitive and lyrical over the years. Still, in designs like those for the Whitaker Center or the Berrie Center, an orthogonal system will be played off against the diagonals of a superimposed grid shift or be cut by a segmental great circle (with its implications of completion and potentials for radial or tangential relationships). The benefits in employing simultaneous planning systems can be legion. A surprisingly dynamic interior can be created within a static shell (New 42nd Street offices); independent volumes can be brought into coordination and axes can be shifted (Creighton University); or relationships beyond the bounds of the building can be established (Texas Christian University). The accidental-seeming residual spaces created by intersecting plan forms and volumes provide special opportunities for animated public areas, like the lobby of the Colburn School, where complex forms provide for a spacious reception area but also offer directional indicators and reductions in scale to create a seamless transition into the workings of the building.

While such plans are generated within intellectual frameworks, HHPA buildings have no need of decoding to be accessible. Ultimately they are designed for direct experience.

Anything else would be out of character for a firm that is notable for its city-bred dedication to the idea of creating environments for lively human interaction, person-to-person and person-to-place. Hierarchies of spaces and functions are evident. Circulation, even in the seemingly most complex plans, operates with clarity. Movement is often governed by distinct, well-marked paths — whether the tubelike connectors at the Salisbury Upper School, the carpet patterns of the Scholastic offices, or the axially cascading escalators of the Los Angeles Public Library — intended to guide the

8

visitor through a dynamic unfolding of the design's rich, varied, and often surprising sequence of changing foci and perceptions. The partners' early and abiding passions for the contemporary arts and for New York City seem to find expression in their penchant for abrupt juxtapositions, potently fragmentary forms, and scenographic manipulations. Fleshed out in three dimensions, HHPA designs are experienced within (as at Bowdoin) and without (as at the Whitaker Center) as articulated but incompleted systems, identifiable but partially concealed masses, colliding forms, casual intersections, interacting levels, expanding and contracting scales. These are designs so complex formally and spatially as to defy neat epitomization and traditional architectural representation. They depend instead, both for study and for communication, on physical and computerized modeling.

9

10

Important for reading such buildings in their collaged complexity are the distinctively patterned and textured surfaces of the juxtaposed components. At LACMA, a striped façade of limestone, green-glazed terracotta, and glass blocks plays off against off-white porcelain-coated steel and the marble mosaic panels of the older pavilions. At the Dance Theatre of Harlem brick contrasts with striped concrete masonry and diaper-patterned polychromed shingling. At the Highland House wooden clapboards mix with red metal shingles, limestone, and granite. Acknowledging an admiration for Bruce Goff's idiosyncratic use of materials and textures, HHPA has established a similar reputation for using ordinary and often inexpensive materials in extraordinary ways. They do so not only to enhance the readability of their forms, but also to establish an appropriate character for the building, to emphasize relationships with context, and to provide sheer sensual pleasure. At first their materials tended to be more industrial, budget restrictions encouraging the use of off-the-shelf components. But claiming they could make architecture out of anything, the partners rendered these materials distinctive by their imaginative applications, as with the combination of stock curtain wall, clay tiles, and prefabricated greenhouse parts in the Columbus (Indiana) Occupational Health Center (1974). As witnessed by the salt dome incorporated into the

11

11. *Columbus Occupational Health Center, entrance view*
12. *San Angelo Museum of Fine Arts and Education Center, stone mock-up*
13. *Spirit Square Arts Center, lobby*
14. *Middlebury College, Center for the Arts, concert hall*
15. *Cleveland Public Library, Louis Stokes Wing, lobby tile wall detail*

3 Goldberger, P. "Brash, Young, and Post-Modern." *New York Times Magazine,* 20 February 1977, p. 26.

12

11

Salisbury Upper School or the runway lighting used as wall fixtures in the Middlebury Center for the Arts, the partners have not lost their taste for placing off-the-shelf components in surprising contexts. The creative use of such low-cost interior and exterior materials as flake board, corrugated industrial siding, clay tile, concrete block, ·cement shingles, and corrugated fiberglass has remained a trademark of the firm. Over time other, more polite materials — metal shingles, granite, architectural terracotta — have entered their vocabulary as well. These, too, are often imbued with something of an unusual or "found" character that makes them extraordinary in their application. The undulating wall at the University of Nebraska in Omaha uses banding of clinker brick from local beehive kilns. The gray granite of the Middlebury Center for the Arts is curb stone. The native Texas limestone for the San Angelo Museum was quarried from an exposed ledge with a remarkable deformed surface. As important as the material is the manner in which it is applied. In an era of perceivably two-dimensional veneers, HHPA surfaces are richly textured and express traditional and sometimes monumental weight and mass. Stone is laid up to feel stony. The standard clay tiles of the façade of Temple Israel are set to create a play of base, quoins, horizontal courses, and vertical flutes. The Roman brick façade of the Colburn School gains in visual interest and substance from periodic shadowed inset coursing.

12

HHPA's interior decoration, rooted in the eclectic and graphically bold tastes of pop culture, is as distinctive and as integral to their designs as is their choice and application of exterior materials. The partnership is famous for its mix of elegant and plebeian materials; emphatically patterned carpets, upholstery, and floor inlays; distinctly colored structural and mechanical systems; bold wall graphics and textures; significant lighting fixtures and animated railings; and historic and contemporary ornamental vocabulary. To eyes accustomed to spare modernist neutrality and coordination in architecture, this taste was a shock in the 1960s and early 1970s. It was called jazzy, funky, retro-chic, pop, and even (by Peter Eisenman) functionalism in drag.[3] Perhaps

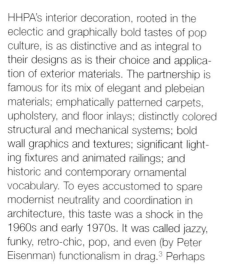

13

less self-consciously strident in recent years, it still has a capacity sometimes to startle. Yet, for its often brash appearance, it is conceived to serve architectural purposes. The intent is more to clarify than to camouflage, to celebrate and enhance one's experience of HHPA buildings and spaces. Decorative juxtapositions further the reading of individual components in a spatial collage like the interior of the Bowdoin Student Center. Color can indicate organization, as with the pervasive blue column grid of the Middlebury Center for the Arts, or serve as locator, as with the multicolored perforated metal ceilings in the shelving areas of the Cleveland Library. Carpet patterns, as in the Scholastic Headquarters, indicate major circulation paths. Inserted elements like the hung ceiling segments in the concert hall of the Colburn School, the arches in the Punahou auditorium and the Brooklyn Academy of Music's Lepercq Space, the oval seating and stage floor in the Middlebury concert hall, and the central pentagon in the sanctuary of Temple Israel, permit focusing and reducing the perceived volume of a large room to establish a sense of intimacy.

14

HHPA also uses decoration to develop a particular character for its designs. At Bowdoin the decor establishes the sense of a cheerful winter-garden interior wrapped around a monumental floor inlay of the college seal. At the Fox Theatres graphics turn the refreshment counter into a segment of a gigantic Fox popcorn tub. At the Punahou School the stage curtain bursts with a custom design of night-blooming cereus. At the Cleveland Library blue-clad columns with exaggerated entasis and a lobby wall profiled like a giant torus moulding topped with a dentil course pay homage in the Stokes Wing to the classical character of the Beaux-Arts main building next door, while a tile frieze of lamps of knowledge announces the concept behind the glowing new structure. That glow is more than a matter of illumination seen through the glass façades; it comes from bold color as well. The lobby wall, for example, is activated with snake-skin-like patterns of blue, yellow, green, and orange conceived to dispel what the architects perceive as the gloom of Cleveland's lakefront weather in favor of warmth and brightness — if also to impart a bit of lively

15

irreverence. Decoration similarly determines character in the concert hall at the Middlebury Center for the Arts, where William Morris wallpapers, a voluptuously overscaled spiraling cherry railing, and sculpted balcony faces impart an overriding elegance to an environment otherwise typified by ground-face cement block, blue steel beams, lacquered flake board, and corrugated fiberglass chandelier-cum-sound-reflectors.

17

Even when its intention is to camouflage, HHPA's decoration is specific and architectural in its purposes. Take the case of Windows on the World in New York. Here the challenge was to reshape the restrictive architectural format of the 106th and 107th floors of the World Trade Center with their vast, low-ceilinged interior spaces and cagelike periphery of too-insistent, too-narrow windows. The goal was to emphasize the stunning views, when they were visible, and to create an interior that could become the occasion itself when they weren't. The architects created variety through the use of curving and folded walls. They animated the very present low ceilings, stepping them up where the floors step down to the periphery and, in the case of the main dining room, treating them like an origami shell carried on folded legs that visually cluster the windows into a broader, more restful and seemingly more penetrable rhythm. They used soft colors that take their cues from those of the surrounding vista at various times of day. In the dining room they kept the palette neutral to focus attention on the views without and on the colorful table settings and food within. Everywhere they reinforced the identity of the place as an aerie looking down on the world with special details — floor inlays of Mercator projection lines, carpets with views of lower Manhattan or the plans of sixteen of the world's famous cities, a Milton Glaser glass bead mural of clouds, Dan Dailey lighting fixtures like illuminated skyscrapers.

18

Although they regularly do significant custom design in such areas as furniture, graphics, lighting fixtures, and carpets, HHPA also readily and successfully incorporate work by other artists into their projects. Thus the chapel in Temple Israel is embellished with Albert Kahn details reused from the congregation's former home, and the

sanctuary focuses on a polychromed steel ark screen commissioned from frequent HHPA collaborator Albert Paley. The Bowdoin Student Center incorporates enlivening supergraphics adapted by Toni Wolf from student-designed stencils. The interiors of Portland's Multnomah County Central Library are embellished according to a "Garden of Knowledge" scheme devised by artist Larry Kirkland. The reading garden at the Cleveland Library features a Maya Lin fountain and Tom Otterness gates, while the interiors of the Stokes Wing include major art installations by eight regional and national artists. The Los Angeles library project incorporates a Lawrence Halprin-designed garden with an embellished water spine by Jud Fine.

13

Another form of collaboration is inherent in HHPA's extensive experience and marked success working with historic buildings. Since the partners' early studies for recycling threatened urban genres like Broadway theaters, movie palaces, and railroad stations and their acclaimed interventions in the interiors of New York's Cooper-Hewitt Museum and the St. Louis Art Museum, they have exhibited a dedication to the idea of continuity in architecture. They neither create buildings of whole cloth in one or another historical vocabulary nor apply arbitrary historic detail in the fashion of much postmodern historicism, but rather produce work that is both inclusively referential and contemporarily grounded. They relish the historic built environment with its rich layering of adaptation over time, and accept its tailoring to present needs as a valid architectural enterprise. In this spirit they essentially take on past builders and architects as collaborators in their contemporary design process, entering into dialogue with their earlier creations while designing in the firm's own voice. This requires a special critical sensitivity to the themes, details, and materials of the past that has made HHPA perhaps the most important single firm today in terms of the restoration and rehabilitation of high-profile public buildings and spaces.

Yet it isn't accurate to call HHPA restoration architects. Their approach to older buildings is pragmatic and creative. They maintain that, given contemporary use expectations, codes, and technologies, it is impossible to

19. *New Amsterdam Theatre, box seats*
20. *New Victory Theater, 42nd Street façade*
21. *Los Angeles County Museum of Art, site plan*
22. *Evo A. DeConcini Federal Building and United States Courthouse, southwest façade*
23. *New York State Historical Association, Fenimore House, American Indian Wing*

4 Diamondstein, B. *American Architecture Now.* New York: Rizzoli, 1980, p. 85.

14

project the life of an historic building through literal restoration. Interpretive intervention always becomes an issue, even in HHPA's purest-seeming projects. Along with their re-creation of such historic details as handrails, lighting, and wainscotting, their work with Stanford University's Main Quadrangle has involved the seismic reinforcement of the stone Romanesque exteriors and the reorganization of interiors to serve new uses and technologies. They reconstructed the exuberant Art Nouveau interior of New York's New Amsterdam Theatre on the basis of historic research. But its appearance also depends on carpeting and fabrics invented in a similar spirit and on the use of an adjusted color scheme — muted to give the appropriately patinated effect of an aged original while taking into account the impact of contemporary lighting — while its function depends on revised access, circulation, technology, and expanded lobby and lounge spaces. Externally, the New Amsterdam has not been restored to its 1903 appearance, but rather retains an Art Deco marquee as a record of its intermediate life as a movie house, an authentic artifact considered more precious by the architects than any re-creation of lost detailing could be. Interpretive decisions in the case of the New Victory Theater have resulted in the acknowledged juxtaposition of three aesthetics — Oscar Hammerstein's original façade and staircase, David Belasco's redecorated interior (both sumptuously restored), and in between a set of unapologetically nonhistoric HHPA lobbies and public amenities.

With so many forms and forces at work in their designs, it is small surprise that HHPA buildings are more frequently perceived as lively experiences than as neat, coherent formal entities. For a firm who early on conceived of architecture as "an attempt to resolve conflicts which are impossible,"[4] refined perfection that turns a building into a formal abstraction is both unattainable and unappealing. Their design approach lends itself to the creation of buildings that are complex, functionally responsive organisms rather than static monuments, addressing the multiplicity of concerns of the moment and often open to the possiblity of adjustment. HHPA has a stated commitment to the ongoing lives of buildings. Thus their

21

19

20

work at LACMA both transformed the original Pereira scheme and accommodated a later pavilion for Japanese art constructed from designs by Bruce Goff. The Fine Arts building at the University of Nebraska at Omaha is organized along a central spine and terminates in a circulation hinge that will permit the future addition of radio and TV departments and a proscenium theater. For the Dance Theatre of Harlem (1994) they expanded their own 1971 adaptation of a preexisting parking garage, inventively transforming the earlier solution to adjust to the altered circumstances of the school. Far from considering preexisting construction an impediment to their aesthetic goals, HHPA accept it as a contributing factor in their design process.

Physical setting also provides a major stimulus for HHPA designs. The broken massing of the Highland House responds to issues of topography, vistas, neighborhood scale, and existing trees. So, too, on a larger scale does the site planning for Soka University, which substitutes for the patrons' initial concept of Beaux-Arts formality an irregular Mediterranean-feeling village with narrow lanes and communal piazzas following the contours of its ridge. The DeConcini Courthouse, in Tucson, is set on its urban site to respond to climate. It maximizes northern and eastern exposures for its offices and wraps south- and west-facing public circulation with sweeping sunscreens. A monumental, canopied but open-air vestibule passes between the wings on a diagonal to join summer (northeast) and winter (southwest) courtyards. The angled disposition of the office units of Ritter Hall at Scripps Institution of Oceanography orients both the offices themselves and the small outdoor rooms defined by their façade toward a newly created campus green space. For the toll plaza at the Rainbow Bridge in Niagara, the surroundings suggested a whole menu of responses: a rainbowlike arc for the bridging office structure, metal detailing to recall the historic bridge, base buildings of the same stone as Niagara Gorge, and a use of patterned glass and trellising to respond to adjacent parklands. The major gallery addition to the Fenimore House in Cooperstown, New York, is constructed beneath garden terraces that create a suitably formal base for the original neo-Georgian house and preserve the vista

23

of sweeping landscape opening to Lake Ostego below. Even more self-effacing is the Vilar Center for the Arts in Beaver Creek, Colorado, where a theater and art gallery have been located entirely below grade, beneath the town-center ice rink and plaza.

The settings for most HHPA works are urban; and for architects who find Manhattan-style urbanism exhilarating in its visual chaos, their own projects demonstrate a notable concern for relating to their built surroundings. The Colburn School in Los Angeles urbanizes its streetscape by relating the alignment, proportions, and rhythms of its façade to those of Arata Isosaki's adjacent MOCA, although the actual materials of its walls, shapes of its roof pavilions, and compactness of its plan are distinctively its own. The Siena on East 76th Street in New York is a high-rise that takes the cues for its massing, horizontal divisions, materials, and details from its neighborhood, melding themes from the landmark church and rectory of St. Jean Baptiste and traditional East Side apartment construction. The library addition at Vassar exemplifies HHPA campus work in the way it seeks to reconcile dissonances of form and vocabulary that have occurred over time. Its placement reinforces the organization of the campus while ceding dominance to the building's older core. Its scale, height, and rhythms echo the Gothic original. Its materials and surface patterns combine themes from the old library with those of diverse neighboring buildings to help integrate the campus aesthetic. The design for the Stokes Wing of the Cleveland Public Library evolved within the tight parameters of the city's 1903 Beaux-Arts "Group Plan," with heights based on those of its two neighbors. Its base relates in terms of scale, masonry, proportions, and classical character to the original library, while an oval plan, a quickened façade rhythm, and glazing dissociate its tower through contrast to assert its own identity and times. Its conception as a separate structure, joined to the older building below grade, preserves and enhances the Eastman Reading Garden, which HHPA (in collaboration with the Olin Partenrship) has given new life as an important open space in downtown Cleveland.

24

25

26

Two other major library/garden projects — New York's Bryant Park and Los Angeles's downtown Public Library — demonstrate the ability of the firm to work with and improve upon existing circumstances. In each case the ultimate success can be credited to HHPA's underlying dedication to the importance of public places within the city and their ability to work creatively and collaboratively with the complex layering of bodies that have authority over such projects. The transformation of Bryant Park (behind the New York Public Library) from a dangerously isolated and underused garden into one of the liveliest and most pleasant oases in mid-town Manhattan involved a fifteen-year commitment and much public dialogue. Working with landscape architect Laurie Olin, HHPA maintained its inherent Beaux-Arts formality, but with improved physical and visual access from the surrounding streets and with the insertion of amenities designed to draw a critical density of activity. Perhaps the greatest challenge was the design of the park restaurant. A steel-and-glass pavilion softened by trellis-work, it establishes a character appropriate to its garden setting and complements the famous rear façade of the library. Dark and low; layered, shadowed, and transparent; decidedly late twentieth century in its technological detailing — it is able to be its own thing without competing against or detracting from its grand marble backdrop.

In Los Angeles, on the other hand, the HHPA work collaborates closely with its historic building. Here the firm dedicated ten years to the challenge of restoring and expanding Bertrand Goodhue's beloved but inefficient and fire-damaged library, exploring some twelve solutions. In the process they collaborated with landscape architect Lawrence Halprin to recreate the Maguire Gardens above a new parking garage, adding a vital and important multiuse outdoor space to the core of the city. For the library itself they rationalized the functions, restored the Goodhue interiors, and appended a major addition. This new Bradley Wing operates as an extension of Goodhue's building in several ways. Physically it extends the central axis of the plan with a monumental new atrium that descends four levels to give light and access to the subterranean floors that

15

27

28. Exxon Service Station
29. Dance Theatre of Harlem, 152nd Street
façade

5 Goldberger, P. "The New Rainbow Room: S'Wonderful." *New York Times,* 20 December 1987, p. 40.
6 Goldberger, "Brash, Young, and Post-Modern." *New York Times Magazine,* 20 February 1977, p. 18.
7 Venturi, R. et al. *Complexity and Contradiction in Architecture.* New York: Museum of Modern Art, 1966, p. 23.

16

made it possible to achieve programmed space without upstaging Goodhue's massing. Stylistically it complements Goodhue's vocabulary, repeating the blocky stuccoed masses and window detailing and introducing architectural terracotta elements in an appropriate spirit. Decoratively it derives its color scheme and motifs from the frescoes of the original building and invents upon them in carpets and furnishings throughout. The original building still feels like Goodhue's, though it has been subtly adjusted for new functions. The Bradley Wing is recognizably contemporary, but celebrates the spirit of the original.

Just as the architects do not always hide their interventions or dogmatically erase the interventions of other times, they also do not shrink from creating in and extending the vocabulary of their models — be they Beaux-Arts, Georgian Revival, Art Nouveau, Art Deco, 1950s Modern, or even (as in the case of the Dance Theatre of Harlem) early HHPA. They have been so successful at capturing the spirit of a place with their own designs that one might be inclined to say of projects like Bryant Park or the Los Angeles Library what critic Paul Goldberger declared about the 1987 HHPA restoration and expansion of the Rainbow Room atop New York's Rockefeller Center: "It is what always should have been there."[5] Given their success with apparently seamless interventions, it may be surprising to realize that this is not always the preferred HHPA approach in historic contexts. Comfortable in their de novo work with the idea of juxtapositions that permit several vocabularies and systems to read at once, they have proposed designs for some historical contexts (e.g., for the Cleveland and Los Angeles libraries) that were more contemporary in character and in stronger contrast with the existing architecture than what eventually was executed. While ultimately patrons and preservation bodies demanded and received more historically literal results than HHPA would initially have been inclined to produce, from the architects' point of view their first proposals had validity in challenging the commissioners and the public to look at their inherited buildings in new ways and in opening up a vital creative dialogue that informed the final design process.

28

29

This is a firm for whom dialogue and challenging parameters are accepted and necessary contributors to making architecture. When not faced with a defined aesthetic (like that at the Los Angeles Library), or economic issues (like those that led to the construction of Philadelphia's Wilma Theater in the core of a new downtown parking garage), or special demands of setting (like those that led to the skewing of the recital hall at Texas Christian University), or historic circumstances (like those at the Punahou School), HHPA seems to come up with its own conditioning parameters. As with its device of looking down on the world's cities at Windows on the World, they often conceptualize a theme for a project. In providing a new identity for LACMA along Wilshire Boulevard, they combined references to the Art Deco glories of commercial Los Angeles with a Busby Berkeley sense of scale and pizzazz. For Soka University, where the founders and educational mission called for an expression of community interaction, they conceived of a hill town with tight building clusters, intimate lanes, and variously shaped piazzas. The architectural vocabulary, in the spirit of Italian towns with twentieth-century interventions, permits a mix of traditional Mediterranean and contemporary aesthetics — a theme supported by drafting-room photo montages of hill-towns, piazzas, vernacular buildings, and street architecture. For the Exxon Service Station at Walt Disney World they created references to shade in the Florida sun — a palm-encircled oasis around a trellised canopy juxtaposed with a louvered Caribbean hut. In other projects motifs have been used that seem to suggest appropriate historical allusions. The Middlebury Center for the Arts is dominated by a great circular courtyard — an allusion to James Stirling's Stuttgart Museum (which in turn refers to Schinkel's iconic Berlin Museum)? The tower of the Stokes Wing at the Cleveland Library is set with tall, square-paned concave bay windows — is their Mackintoshian character a reference to the great library of the Glasgow School of Art? The Dance Theatre of Harlem, which is topped with a weather vane in the form of Arthur Mitchell, is also faced with insistent black and white horizontal stripes — a reference to Adolf Loos' famous project for a house for Josephine Baker?

These must be posed as questions, because the architects aren't saying. They have always maintained that they would rather build than talk. They do not wish to be pinned down. As Hardy expressed it early on, "We have always felt strongly that we should not issue a manifesto, telling the world our work represents six holy ideas. If you do that, you become imprisoned by it."[6] This is not to say, though, that the ideas do not exist within the work. They abound — surprising, pushing boundaries, entertaining. Robert Venturi and others have made connections between postmodern attitudes in architecture and sixteenth-century Italian Mannerism. There is much analogous. In both cases a sophisticated generation of architects responded to the challenge of a refined design mode (High Renaissance, International Style Modernism) that they found to be unrealistic in its narrow vocabulary and abstract idealism. They pursued impure but liberating and creative patterns of rule-breaking, often clothing it in supreme wit. Until recent years history has judged Mannerist architects (with few exceptions) as clever and sometimes perverse lightweights, somehow lacking in seriousness. Only through postmodern eyes have they begun to be seen once again as remarkably intelligent and inventive creative artists, expanding their art to include issues of exisiting conditions, contrasting purposes, experiential manipulation, and expressive communication (e.g., malaise, humor). Like the Mannerists, HHPA ran the risk of being assessed as less serious than it is. The partners have not helped people to define and categorize them either aesthetically or theoretically. They have developed no easily identifiable look and have tended to get uneasy when critically associated too closely with one or another contemporary movement. They have pursued the grayness of complexity and contradiction, but not also the literary exposition of the fact. They have not allied themselves with any theoretical camp. They have avoided a stance of self-seriousness, revelling in what might be considered impurity and popular accessibility. They have indulged openly in cleverness and wit and have cheerfully admitted to having fun.

Rather than grand composers, HHPA tends to come across as virtuoso jazz musicians — embellishing and improvising brilliantly and delightfully on their given themes.

30

31

32

The themes themselves are serious architectural issues of our times: urban context, individual experience, public interaction, adaptive use, restoration, institutional identity, cultural resources, complex functional programs. The approaches they bring to them represent a full range of mainstream postmodern concerns as articulated by the theorists and critics. They have been participants, creative users, and important innovators in "both-and,"[7] the hybrid rather than the pure, ambiguity rather than clarity, messy vitality rather than unity, visual pluralism, contextualism, historical quotation, high-tech vocabulary, pop imagery, applied decoration, allusion, multivalence, rationalist geometries, and deconstructed forms. They address their work to a broad public audience. The genres in which they work connect with the public experience in direct and significant ways, providing late–twentieth-century America with a remarkable set of revitalized cultural monuments and memorable public spaces. The spirit they impart to all of this is one of creative celebration. The result is a set of buildings, few of which ultimately may be isolated as timeless abstract monuments but all of which are vital expressions of their times within the architectural continuum. While they appeal directly to experience, these are also buildings charged with lessons for anyone who is serious about the creative challenges of making architecture in the late twentieth century.

This volume, dedicated to the work of the 1990s, is full of those lessons. It contains a richly instructive fragment of HHPA production, full of connections to past work (continuing concerns, bits of vocabulary, lessons learned), and imbued with potential for what is still to come. Like an HHPA plan, this body of work is not necessarily a closed system. It might best be perceived as the architects did their designs for LACMA, the Dance Theatre of Harlem, or the Fine Arts Building at the University of Nebraska at Omaha — as telling pieces of a larger and evolving master plan, ready to be expanded in a new fashion but also with reference to and building off of what went before. These designs of Hardy Holzman Pfeiffer Associates in their prime years provide a significant and mature slice of a career that can best be seen as an ongoing study in the exhilaration of diverse architectual creation.

BUILDINGS AND INTERIORS

BRYANT PARK RESTORATION AND BRYANT PARK GRILL AND BP CAFÉ

New York, New York, 1992, 1995

20 Bryant Park has undergone several major transformations in its 160-year history. In the 1930s, Robert Moses, the New York City Commissioner of Parks, changed the English country garden landscape into a formal beaux-arts square. To insulate it from the hustle and bustle of midtown Manhattan, he raised the park four feet above street level, adding steps for access and planting hedges and trees to muffle traffic noise. Over the years this visual and physical remoteness deterred public use of the park; it fell into disrepair and became an enclave for drug dealing and other misuse.

In 1980 the New York Public Library and the Rockefeller Brothers Fund established the Bryant Park Restoration Corporation (BPRC), a nonprofit organization, which, with the City of New York, undertook to restore this landmark. Owned by the City, the park is managed by the BPRC with revenue from the Building Improvement District, from rent paid by commercial ventures in the park, and from the city itself.

To test the urban analyst William H. Whyte's premise that the introduction of pedestrian amenities combined with open access and places to sit would increase public enjoyment of the park, HHPA was commissioned to build two temporary kiosks on the New York Public Library's Fifth Avenue terrace. After it had been repopulated, the BPRC sought to apply Whyte's theory on a larger scale, behind the library, in the park itself. Two food kiosks were placed on its east side, while, on its west terrace, restrooms, a park maintenance house, and the Bryant Park Grill and Café, which flank the William Cullen Bryant monument, were added.

HHPA, working with the landscape architect Laurie Olin and the garden designer Lynden B. Miller, further proved Whyte's hypothesis, reclaiming the park for the public. Their design restored the raised terraces paved with bluestone and granite, planted with bosks of sycamore trees surrounding a great lawn. Miller created a 300-foot-long flower border, along the north and south sides of the lawn, which constitute an entire

1. View east toward Bryant Park Grill

crosstown block and two of the nation's longest perennial borders. This visual drama shifts with the seasons.

Reversing some of the changes made by Moses, HHPA added new entrances and ramps to the north and south, and altered existing access points to encourage easy visitation. To further draw pedestrian traffic, hedges were removed and openings were made in the central lawn's balustrade. These modifications, with the new dining facilities and informal seating areas, brought the park back to life, as a resting place, source of inspiration, and new and immensely popular venue for events such as fashion shows and film screenings.

The restaurant and café allow more than 1400 patrons to dine inside, outside, and on the roof. These delicate-looking buildings feature lattice pavilions with an abundance of natural plantings to blend with the landscape. Like the kiosks nestled among the trees in other parts of the square, they are reminiscent of Parisian parks' decorative tradition. The one-story restaurant, conceived as a leafy bower, offers uninterrupted views of the outdoors; its composition, an inner layer of glass and steel and an outer layer of woven aluminum and weathered-wood trelliswork, supports wisteria vines and large flower boxes.

When it opened, in 1993, the project was hailed as a "small miracle" by *Time* magazine, and was honored with both the AIA Honor Award for Urban Design and the Urban Land Institute's Award for Excellence. The introduction of amenities, careful interventions in the landscape, and proper maintenance have made the park a safe, tranquil, year-round urban oasis. One of the finest examples of public-private partnership, it has become a favorite spot for tourists, office workers, library patrons, and city dwellers alike.

2. *Aerial view*
3. *Bryant Park Grill elevation*
4. *Site plan*
5. *Southeast view*
6. *Kiosks on corner of 42nd Street and Sixth Avenue*

2

3

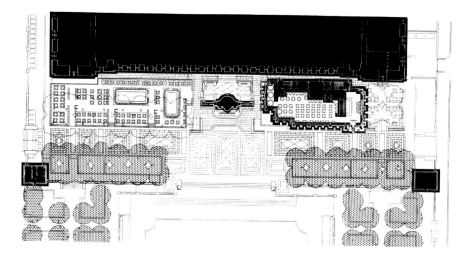

4

25   50   100

5

6

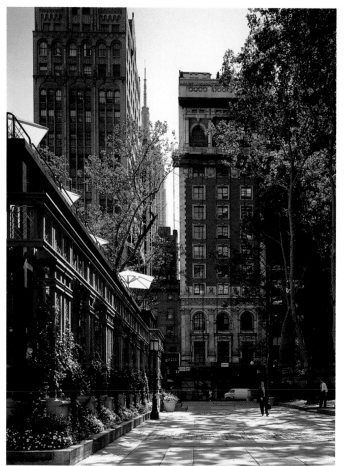

7

8

9

10

11

7. View toward 40th Street
8. View toward 42nd Street
9. BP Café next to the monument
of William Cullen Bryant
10. BP Café
11. Bryant Park Grill, south façade
12. Trellis detail

12

CENTER FOR THE ARTS

Middlebury College
Middlebury, Vermont, 1992

26 In 1987 HHPA was commissioned to design new facilities for the performing and visual arts at Middlebury College, one of the oldest and most highly regarded liberal arts institutions in the country. The initial effort, to create additions to existing campus structures, later evolved into a new 100,000-square-foot Center for the Arts, which houses an art gallery and the departments of theater, music, and dance. The building provides a single focal point accessible to both the Middlebury community and the general public.

After the Arts Master Plan was developed, an appropriate site was identified on the southern edge of this pastoral Vermont campus, near its admissions, athletic, and library buildings. To assure that the center would be visually congruent with its scenic setting among the Green Mountains, an expansive building with a low profile was designed. In consolidating the arts programs within one facility care was taken to give each department its own identity while providing common social spaces for artistic cross-fertilization. The building is inset and overlaid with square, circular, and octagonal forms that represent each of the major program elements.

Stone was used on the exterior in response to the nineteenth-century limestone and marble buildings on campus. Massive rough-cut blocks of pink granite clad the entrance-way and concert hall. Gray split-faced granite encloses the Museum of Art, the dance studio, and the black-box theater. These forms are woven together by a common skin of traditional New England clapboard and distinct standing seam copper roof.

A multilevel circulation space serves as the lobby and reception area. A segmented stairway and bridges provide access to all activities, minimizing the traditional use of corridors. Carefully placed windows and openings allow visitors to peek into rehearsal and performance areas from the lobby. Daylight filters through skylights and adds warmth to the rich blend of stone, wood, steel, and clapboard.

1. North façade
2. Detail of stone and clapboard juncture
3. Courtyard with Dan Graham sculpture
4. Main level plan

1

2

3

4

25 50   100

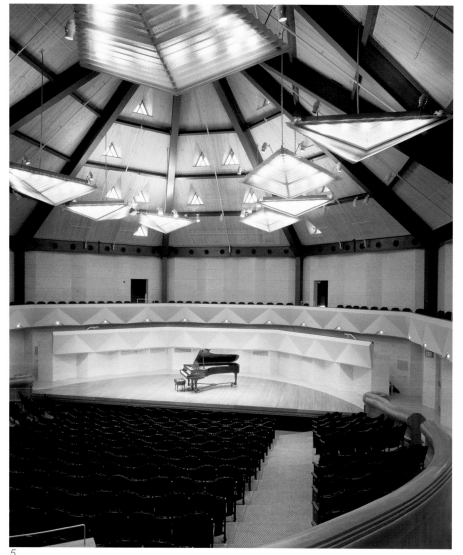

5

7

6

After extensive programming discussions involving the faculty, various arts departments, and the board of trustees, it became evident that community use was an integral part of the center's mission. More than 250 public events occur there yearly. At the same time, it was critical to maintain the personal quality of teacher-student interaction that flourishes in smaller environments. To facilitate both public and academic needs, exhibition and performance spaces were designed to be flexible. The museum allows faculty to conduct slide presentations and display works from the permanent collection within the study gallery/seminar room. To enhance intimacy in the 370-seat concert hall, the audience and performers are embraced by a single balcony that surrounds the orchestra and drawn together under a steeply pitched roof. Adaptable lighting and configuration within the black-box theater and dance studio accommodate performance, practice, or instruction.

The college achieved its goal of visually substantiating its commitment to the arts by including administration, production, teaching, research, and support spaces for all of the arts within one center, encouraging the integrative thinking inherent in a liberal arts institution. The center's inviting interior spaces and plentiful use of stone were achieved for $162 per square foot.

5. Concert hall
6. Dance rehearsal room
7. Concert hall rail detail
8. Studio theater
9. Dance theater

8

9

30

10

11

10. Upper level lobby
11. Upper level lobby
12. Gallery

THE NEW 42ND STREET INC. OFFICES

New York, New York, 1992

32 The New 42nd Street Inc. is a nonprofit organization dedicated to revitalizing the dilapidated theaters on West 42nd Street. HHPA designed their offices, on the 23rd floor of the landmark McGraw-Hill Building, well before the future of these theaters was known. The goal was to transform 4000 feet of raw space into a charismatic workplace where employees could focus on their momentous mission — all for $85 per square foot.

A meticulous manipulation of space, color, and lighting and an innovative use of natural and recycled materials echo the diverse and vibrant urban environment of 42nd Street itself. To create circulation patterns appropriate to the organization's theatrical objectives, HHPA began with a deliberate departure from the conventional rectangular floor plan. Clusters of cubicles, placed on inexpensive sisal carpeting, were oriented on angles to energize the space.

Visitors are greeted in an entry area that features a luminescent reception desk set against rhythmically striped panels of oriented strand board. Opposite, a collage of black-and-white photographs of the street's historic theaters is mounted on a canted wall.

Six semiprivate staff areas are furnished with pink anegre desks supported by wrought-iron, nineteenth-century-style table bases, contemporary swiveling chairs upholstered in a pink tapestry pattern turned inside out, and 1930s lamps rescued from an East Village thrift shop. The director's corner space, the only private office, offers prospective sponsors an enticing view of the theaters below.

The New 42nd Street Inc.'s offices honor the history and promise of this renowned district with a spirited and economical office interior of great flexibility and spatial variety.

1. Reception area

2

2. HHPA collage of historic 42nd
Street theater photographs
3. Floor plan
4. Private office
5. Semiprivate staff areas

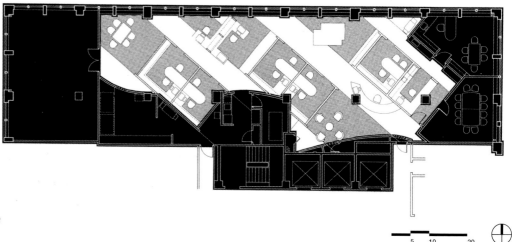

3

5   10   20

4

5

DEL AND LOU ANN WEBER
FINE ARTS BUILDING

University of Nebraska at Omaha
Omaha, Nebraska, 1992

36   The University of Nebraska at Omaha's
new Fine Arts Building marked the first time
in the school's eighty-year history that the
building committee had selected a non-
Nebraska firm for a design project. At the
time of awarding the commission, UNO's
campus consisted of mostly brick buildings,
none of which reflected its adventuresome
arts programs. David Shrader, a musician
and the dean of the fine arts program,
performed at the Hult Center for Performing
Arts in Eugene, Oregon (designed by HHPA
in 1982), and was particularly impressed with
the quality of that space. The goal, to have a
noteworthy facility that physically represented
the arts, led to the selection of HHPA and
the Schemmer Associates of Omaha.

1. *Main entrance from parking*
2. *Ground level plan*
3. *East façade*

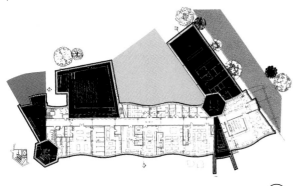

1

15 30   60

2

4

As was done at Middlebury College, a building was designed that, in giving new focus to the arts, is also in keeping with existing campus architecture. The four-story building is finished in a variety of masonry materials visually compatible with those used elsewhere on campus, including the recently constructed campanile. Clinker bricks manufactured in one of the few remaining beehive kilns in Omaha constitute the bulk of the building, which houses classrooms and labs; Minnesota limestone clads its north and south towers; while South Dakota granite envelops the theater and gallery. Each form is topped by a metal roof; the smaller elements have shingles, while the longitudinal section features a vaulted roof and clerestory.

The building design responds to the natural constraints of the steeply sloping site, and to the practical nature of the master plan for this urban university. It develops the south side of an exterior plaza and anchors the west end of campus. Undulating walls foreshorten and articulate its 300-foot length while establishing an interior link between the parking area and the main pedestrian campus mall. A series of windows punctuate the interior double-loaded corridors, revealing to passersby the art and drama activities within. The art gallery's location near the foyer invites pedestrians from the mall to glimpse exhibitions.

The linear arrangement of teaching, lab, and office spaces creates a spine along which varied geometric elements are appended. Hexagonal towers house faculty and student lounges to the north, and provide a circulation hinge to the south, to which a future addition is possible. The trapezoidal experimental theater and rectangular gallery wing veer off the building's west side and shape a new sculpture garden open to the campus. A multistory lobby to the north completes the 78,500-square-foot composition.

Dr. Shrader sees HHPA's design as giving high visibility to the arts both inside and out, while lending strong organizing elements to the campus' newer west quad. The building's mix of texture, color, and form was accomplished for $117 per square foot.

4. Art studio
5. Experimental theater
6. Costume shop
7. Art gallery

6

7

40

8

10

11

12

8. Lobby stair
9. Doorway detail
10. Minnesota limestone detail
11. South Dakota granite detail
12. Clinker bricks
13. Site plan
14. Entrance from main campus walkway

9

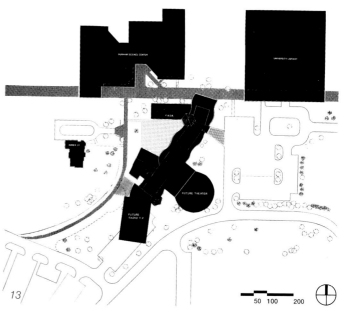

13

50 100 200

FOX THEATRES
Wyomissing, Pennsylvania, 1993

42   The design of the Fox movie theater complex in Wyomissing, Pennsylvania, provides as much entertainment as the cinematic productions it screens. Though it is located in a suburb of Reading, the building has all the dazzle of Hollywood. However, unlike the excesses frequently associated with show business, the design was realized for $62 per square foot. Economical construction materials and systems allowed the project to maintain tight budget constraints without stripping the building of its visual impact.

Poised at the curve of an elliptical drive on an 8½-acre site, the theater sits on a black-and-white striped plaza made of alternating bands of concrete and asphalt, with geometric planting beds on either side of the main entry. Illuminated poster cases on pedestals line the drive. The 30,000-square-foot complex is divided into two parts: the theaters and the lobby. Eight theaters are grouped into a simple L-shaped volume covered in massive, corrugated galvanized siding. Against this backdrop an upturned roof shelters a glass-walled lobby.

Fox's vibrant lobby showcases a towering boxoffice that intersects its roof plane and serves as a beacon to all moviegoers. A conical concession stand, seductively reminiscent of a huge tub of popcorn, is emblazoned with Fox-style tickets in bright colors. A rectilinear brick box contains the restrooms. To enhance orientation and visual interest, each of these program elements contrasts with the others in shape and material. Metal ductwork, columns, and

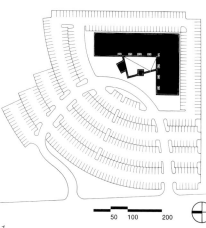

1

1. Site plan
2. Entrance

beams are exposed, and are accented with a vigorous color palette. Sections of the exterior glass wall are coated with colored films. Floral-patterned carpeting promotes an interesting dialogue with the building's otherwise industrial character.

With a total of 1600 seats, the eight theaters range in size from a 400-seat auditorium to an intimate 100-seat asymmetrical screening room. All viewing areas were individually designed with the importance of good sightlines in mind, maximum screen size, and layouts with minimum seating distance to the screen. Each is equipped with the newest technology in film projection and sound amplification. The theaters' blue and orange seats have cup holders and high backs. Even better, they provide enough room for people to go to the middle of a row without making it necessary for those already seated to stand.

The dynamic interplay of lights, colors, patterns, and forms activates the theater complex and heightens the cinematic experience. All the comforts of contemporary theater are provided in a zestful setting that is both affordable and engaging.

A planned addition would increase the number of screens to fourteen. Design concepts include extending the L-shape configuration or spooning the new cinemas against the existing theaters. After the Fox Theatres construction was completed the new administrative offices were designed within an existing building overlooking the theaters. Interior elements such as vibrant yellow cubicles on angle and a massive glass wall reflect gestures in the movie complex across the way.

3. Lobby
4. Detail of lobby ceiling
5. 220-seat cinema
6. Ground floor plan
7. Concession stand

3

4

5

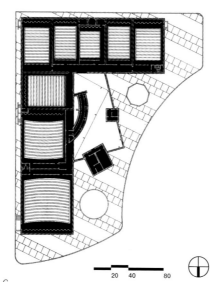

20   40   80

6

LOS ANGELES PUBLIC LIBRARY: CENTRAL LIBRARY

Los Angeles, California, 1993

1. Tom Bradley Wing
2. First floor plan
3. South façade of Goodhue building

46 When the Central Library opened in 1926, it was the most significant civic building in Los Angeles. Its design, by Bertram Grosvenor Goodhue, was progressive in spirit, without specific relation to any defined historical style. Almost square in plan, a grand central rotunda was wrapped with tiers of book stacks surrounded by light-filled reading rooms. As the focus of surrounding downtown development, the library's access was highly democratic, and there were entrances on all four sides. Gardens flanking the building to the east and west provided a welcome oasis. Goodhue's achievement included the inte–gration of artwork throughout the building, from exterior sculptures and inscriptions to interior ceiling stenciling and murals.

By the late 1960s, the building had become derelict from deferred maintenance, difficult to use, and an eyesore. The original layout left no room for the expansion of collections, and books were literally stuffed into overcrowded shelving. No central air conditioning, no fire suppression systems, and poor illumination furthered this civic landmark's fall from grace. In 1969 the city demolished the walkways, pools, fountains, and trees of the library's magnificent west lawn, to make way for additional parking. Throughout the 1970s, proposals to demolish the building and develop the site were made to the City Council.

Fortunately, the library was spared demolition as the result of valiant efforts by planners, developers, architects, and preservationists. In 1983 HHPA was chosen to develop a comprehensive plan to update and expand the existing 225,000-square-foot library. Twelve design options were explored ranging from an underground addition to a freestanding high-rise. The selected scheme positions a partially underground addition on the site of the former children's wing, to the east of the Goodhue structure. This careful siting preserved the preeminence of the original building and enabled the recreation of the west lawn.

In 1986 while design work was proceeding, the library suffered two fires by arson and a year later an earthquake, all of which caused considerable damage. With

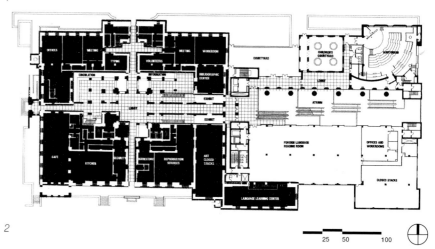

1

2

25   50   100

4

5

historians and art conservation experts, HHPA devised ways to restore and protect artworks, recapture original colors, and re-create historic light fixtures. On the exterior, layers of paint were removed from the original cement plaster-and-limestone façade, and surfaces were patched and repaired. The building's distinguishing exterior feature, a pyramidal spire clad in brilliantly-colored decorative tiles and topped with a torch symbolizing the "light of learning," was exquisitely restored.

The renovated original building now houses the library functions frequently used by visitors: the popular library, children's literature, the circulation desk, and information services, as well as rare books, administration and support services, and several new public meeting rooms. Its focus is still a day-lit rotunda, now fully restored.

In designing the new 330,000-square-foot Tom Bradley Wing, the original landmark's prominence in the skyline was retained by placing more than half of the new addition below street level. The central feature of the wing is a dramatic, glass-roofed, eight-story atrium. With its green terracotta tile columns and its extensive use of commissioned art, the space is a modern counterpart to Goodhue's central rotunda. Escalators in the atrium lead to each of the library's seven subject departments, which house the heart of the collection.

The exterior of the wing was inspired by Goodhue's original design, with blocklike massing and asymmetrical façades. Figurative sculpture, which softened the austere original, is translated into faceted tile pilasters in the new. Windows are proportioned and patterned to echo those in the historic building, and the exterior finish materials include smooth stuccolike coating, decorative copper roof elements, and a distinctive green terracotta tile. The relationship between the two structures is sympathetic and interpretive,

4. Maguire Gardens
5. Tom Bradley Wing, east façade
6. Existing conditions before re-creation of west lawn
7. Axial spine leading to west entry with artwork by Jud Fine

6

an acknowledgment of the transformation of a once neglected architectural icon into a major civic resource for the twenty-first century.

Goodhue's colorful and decorative features were carried forward in HHPA's design of interior elements, with new furniture, carpets, and lighting matching the standard of the original detail and decor. Motifs, patterns, and colors found in the resplendent stenciled ceilings and murals of the historic building were translated into new, contemporary designs. Original light fixtures documented in Goodhue's drawings served as models for accurate reproductions or as elements incorporated into new pole and pendant fixtures.

The community spaces throughout the facility give the building much of its spirit. The 240-seat Mark Taper Auditorium, with its associated lobby and courtyards, is in demand for conferences, performances, readings, and awards ceremonies. Outside, the new Robert F. Maguire III Gardens top a 942-space underground parking garage. This 1½-acre park, designed by the landscape architect Lawrence Halprin as part of HHPA's master plan for the site, features an indoor-outdoor restaurant, an informal amphitheater, new fountains, and commissioned works of art. Some 160 new trees dot the lawns, with blue Italian Cypress lining the central approach. A desirable addition to Los Angeles's dense downtown, the garden plays a significant role in the city's overall revitalization effort.

The renovation and expansion of the Central Library, the largest in the western United States, took a decade to complete and involved approvals by more than twenty city, state, and federal agencies. On opening day, more than 80,000 patrons rejoiced in the splendor of new and restored facilities. Cause for celebration goes beyond new state-of-the-art technology and expanded services and programs to the preservation of an important historic monument for public use in a city largely defined by new construction and private spaces.

8. *Restored historic rotunda*
9. *Refinished zodiac chandelier*
10. *Public event staged in atrium*
11. *Atrium*

8

9

10

12

13

14

15

16

17

12. Restored children's reading room
13. Children's puppet theater
14. New subject department reading room
15. Mark Taper Auditorium
16. Detail of auditorium
17. Fabric detail

SCHOLASTIC INC. HEADQUARTERS

New York, New York, 1993

54　The dynamic, state-of-the-art headquarters of the publisher Scholastic Inc. occupies two buildings which were former manufacturing lofts. Scholastic wanted an environment that would promote social interaction among workers in different departments, have spaces that would be easily reconfigured as priorities and technologies change, and convey the company's progressive approach to publishing. Conceptually, the commission was an enhancement of HHPA's design approach employed when the firm first consolidated all of Scholastic's departments into a converted industrial warehouse in 1983.

Scholastic's new home, in the historic SoHo cast-iron district, accommodates publishing divisions of various sizes, corporate offices, conference rooms, a library, and support spaces. Employee amenities include a health/fitness area in the basement and a greenhouse dining space on the roof offering spectacular views of lower Manhattan.

A steadily evolving office structure led to the creation of a variety of workspaces, including semiprivate offices and a series of open work stations with custom furniture partitions that can be readily changed. Partition walls vary in height, depending on the degree of privacy needed, and are staggered to act as sound diffusers. Circulation corridors are positioned alongside window walls so that all employees can enjoy natural light and city vistas. Each floor invites exploration. Doors and walls are painted in a palette of pastels, arranged in a random medley. The main circulation carpet is emblazoned with the company's creed, columns are painted Scholastic's signature red, and patterns of exposed mechanical ducts and cable trays invigorate the space and provide easy access for changing technologies.

All fourteen floors are connected by what has been called "a periscope of natural light" — a ten-story atrium whose mirrors reflect light up and down its colorful, offset stairwell. The spaciousness of the light-filled circulation spine encourages casual

1. Building exterior along Broadway
2. Second floor/library plan
3. Atrium stairwell

1

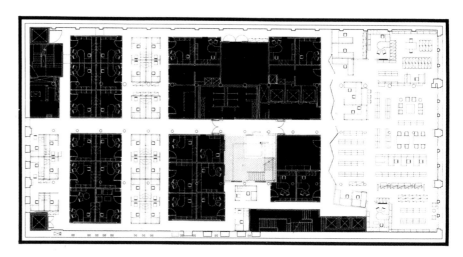

2

5　10　　30

4

5

exchanges among employees. Arrival from the street is on the fifth floor, and the main reception area, conference rooms, and executive offices are on the building's sixth floor, which makes the stairwell an attractive option for access to upper and lower levels.

The third floor holds the company's vast library, an area that features a playful, zig-zag wall of glass. It also provides open-stack facilities for casual reading, private carrels for research activities, and a separate video research/screening room. The top floor of the building has a lively employee dining hall placed in an attractive, greenhouse setting. Cafeteria and private dining areas accommodate 200 people and a rooftop terrace permits a wide range of warm weather events.

Behind this nineteenth-century façade, a sophisticated and flexible twenty-first-century electronic workplace meets the challenges of a company now in the forefront of the ever-changing publishing industry.

4. Company creed woven into circulation carpet
5. Private offices
6. Penthouse dining room

HIGHLAND HOUSE

Madison, Wisconsin, 1993

58   Named after the neighborhood it occupies in Madison, Highland House comprises seven polygonal structures, connected by arc-shaped meridians that allude to Italian hilltop villas. Each element of this small village was carefully sited and sculpted to relate to its landscape, protecting neighbors' views and preserving the topography. Only one of the thirty trees on the property was removed. Special preconstruction measures were taken to protect an American chestnut tree, one of the few surviving examples of this species found in Wisconsin.

To provide a healthy environment, the building frame is made from solid wood sections. No glued, treated, or synthetic structural pieces were used. Design elements include sun-dried floor tiles and wooden floors to minimize dust and carpets. During construction, care was taken to use products that emit low levels of gas from paints, stains, sealers, sealants, and insulation. The exterior materials are also natural.

The connecting meridians are covered with red metal shingles that set them apart from the other structures, which are sheathed in granite, limestone, and wood clapboard. Towers and vivid rooflines define the massing and are fenestrated to permit generous natural interior light and panoramas of earth, sky, and, in winter, Lake Mendota. The

1. *Minnesota stone chimney*
2. *North façade*
3. *South façade*

2, 3

1

4

4. Kitchen
5. Meridian
6. First floor plan
7. Dining room

windows are positioned to frame specific views and take advantage of solar orientation.

The octagonal kitchen is the nerve center of the house. Radiating from it are a living room and library proportioned to a golden section, a pentagonal dining room with the master bedroom on the second floor, a hexagonal guesthouse, and a multitiered garage topped by an observation tower. These areas are discrete; they can be closed off, and their mechanical systems can be operated as they are needed.

A deeply saturated color palette and extensive millwork define each room. The master bedroom features a domed mural inspired by the Paris Opera House and painted by decorative artists at the Conrad Schmidt Studios. In the living room, lighting fixtures are inverted lampshades. A studio on the third floor of the hexagon is an enclave for painting.

As opposed to designing a home within one large mass, this assemblage of forms both preserves its environment and nurtures its residents' personal style of living. The house accepts the qualities of several unconventional architectural building types, most notably a tree house, an old stone castle, and a woodland cabin.

5

1 ENTRY
2 MERIDIAN
3 LIVING
4 LIBRARY
5 DINING
6 KITCHEN
7 GLASS PORCH
8 GARAGE
9 GUEST ROOM
10 MASTER BEDROOM
11 MASTER DRESSING
12 TOWER
13 STUDIO

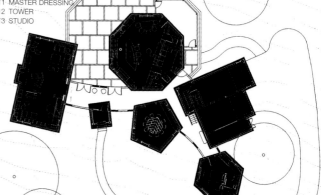

6

10   20   40

EVERETT CENTER

Dance Theatre of Harlem
New York, New York, 1994

1. West façade
2. Corridor detail
3. Stair detail
4. Building façade along 152nd Street

62 In 1968, Arthur Mitchell, the former New York City Ballet principal and a disciple of George Balanchine, opened a small ballet school in the basement of a Harlem church. In its first three years the Dance Theatre of Harlem (DTH) attracted more than 400 students, and HHPA was commissioned to convert a two-story parking garage, on 152nd Street and Amsterdam Avenue, into dance studios and administrative offices.

Over the next two decades DTH became internationally known for both its accredited school of dance, attended by some 1300 students, and its professional ballet company, with a repertoire of seventy-five works and an extensive touring schedule. In 1990 HHPA was asked to design much-needed additional space.

A new building to the west of the garage houses the school's main dance studio, classrooms, parents' lounge, offices, and a second-floor terrace for small gatherings. The completed project enabled DTH to consolidate its operations, which had been scattered around the city, and reinforced its artistic and economic commitment to the Harlem area. Though DTH is a long-established neighborhood constituent, the vibrant design of its school reflects its energy and venturous spirit, setting it apart from nearby tenements and municipal buildings.

The juxtaposition of dissimilar architectural forms and materials — red brick, multicolor shingles set into a diamond pattern, and black and white bands of masonry — creates dramatic streetfront presence. Consistent brick configurations and window treatments were used throughout to visually connect new and old. The converted garage now appears as one of a collage of elements that invigorate the whole.

Further accentuating DTH's progressive outlook is its bold interior scheme. A palette of earth tones highlighted with intense colors, brings the facility to life, as do the custom carpeting and terrazzo tile floors that mark its circulation pathways. The primary dance studio features a translucent glass wall that permits abundant natural light. A great curving roof, seen from the

1

2

3

5

6

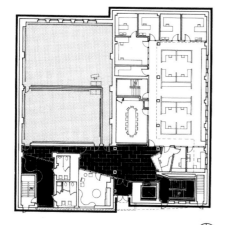

7

street, alludes to the room's massive scale. Skylights and interior glazing within the offices provide an airy and open working environment.

The interplay of texture, form, and geometry, inside and out, is meant to inspire choreographic investigation and collaboration among students and teachers. It also calls attention to the power of the positive activity generated by DTH, locally and around the world.

5. Main dance studio facing south
6. Lobby
7. First floor plan
8. Main dance studio facing east

10 20   40

DILLINGHAM HALL

Punahou School
Honolulu, Hawaii, 1994

66 The challenge posed by the restoration and expansion of the historic Dillingham Hall was preserving the building's architectural character while upgrading the theater to contemporary standards. Designed by Bertram Goodhue in 1924, and completed after his death by Hardie Philip in 1929, the theater has been in continual use since the day it opened. Dillingham Hall was originally an auditorium that also functioned as the preparatory school's chapel. In 1967 its use moved towards various types of proscenium stage presentations including music and drama events. For twenty years prior to renovation the makeshift theater housed highly sophisticated student productions including performances by an orchestra so skilled it recently performed at Carnegie Hall.

Dillingham Hall is one of many low-rise buildings designed by Goodhue on the island of Oahu. Perhaps as a result of his not having lived to see its completion, the theater did not resemble Goodhue's other work, known for its rich detail and surface decoration. By contrast, the theater is considered one of his most minimal of buildings. Its exterior of white stucco and its green clay-tile roof were complemented by an almost exclusively off-white interior scheme.

As part of the renovation, HHPA added layers of contemporary ornament to essentially complete the room with respect to Goodhue's legacy. A vigorous palette of tropical green and blue was introduced in bold geometric patterned upholstery, textured carpeting, custom-designed stage curtain with night-blooming cereus motif, and new technical arches and mechanical stanchions.

Six structural parabolic arches made of concrete define the theater's ceiling plane. These were supplemented with three pairs of deep blue steel arches within alternating bays. Catwalks for house lights, technical lighting, sound systems, and other production equipment are suspended below. An acoustical reflector made of Hawaiian koa wood is mounted to the arch positioned over the stage.

Seating for 653 patrons was reconfigured on the orchestra floor, and the balcony was repitched to improve sightlines. A new parterre narrows the auditorium, enhances

1

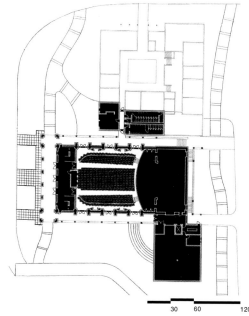

2

30 60   120

1. Restored exterior with new addition
2. Main level plan
3. Existing auditorium conditions

3

4

6

5

room acoustics for symphonic performances, and allows wheelchair access. An expanded stage is equipped with a mechanized pit lift, which can be elevated to make room for the chorus, or lowered to accommodate the orchestra.

Prior to renovation, Dillingham Hall was ventilated by open windows. Heat, humidity, dust, and noise interfered with performances and audience comfort. To alleviate these problems new air-conditioning systems were concealed in acoustically treated, vertical air-supply stanchions. These eight towers, in varying heights up to 26 feet, are positioned along the perimeter of the room as decorative elements. Large illuminated steel globes atop each cylinder augment house lighting.

On the exterior, the traditional Hawaiian-style double sloped roof was recovered with mission-barrel tiles supplied by the same manufacturer as the originals. Redwood windows, doors, and pergolas were replaced, conforming to Goodhue's design. A new annex adds faculty offices and increases workspace and storage for scenery and costumes. Its design balances an earlier administrative addition located on the opposite side of the stage house.

Supported by the commitment of the Punahou School and the generosity of donors, the restored Dillingham Hall is now an appropriate setting for the caliber of performance achieved by students of this distinguished school.

4. Auditorium orchestra and balcony seating
5. Air-supply stanchions/access to catwalks
6. Detail of parabolic arch
7. View toward proscenium
with pit elevator raised

DAVID SAUL SMITH UNION

Bowdoin College
Brunswick, Maine, 1995

1. Oversized stone detail at entry
2. View from third floor of Jack Magee's Pub
3. First floor plan
4. Reconstituted façade

1

70 In the summer of 1992, HHPA was invited to make a presentation at Bowdoin College about converting the 1912 gymnasium, Hyde Cage, into a student union. Among the questions HHPA was asked to address was: How can tradition and innovation achieve a balance to make the campus center very much a part of Bowdoin but at the same time create a new and invigorating addition to campus life?

The answer came in the design of the facility, renamed the David Saul Smith Union, as testament that tradition and innovation can coexist harmoniously. Founded in 1794 as the first college in what would eventually become Maine, Bowdoin is steeped in tradition. Its buildings document the evolution of architectural styles over the past 200 years. This visual chronology remains an integral part of the college's identity. Though Hyde Cage was not considered one of Bowdoin's architectural jewels, launching its adaptive reuse was an opportunity to honor its history.

In 1928 the then all-male college built Moulton Union to accommodate its 700 students. By 1992 enrollment had reached more than 1500, and new places for student activities were greatly needed. It was decided that Moulton would remain the formal room on campus, while Smith would be its family room.

In surveys students expressed their yearning for respite during the long, gray days of winter, and this building lent itself admirably to transformation to a winter garden. From the outside, one gets little sense that Hyde Cage has been modified. A new double-height entrance framed by large granite blocks and fanciful paving leading up to it merely hint at its radical interior conversion. The distinct character of the original interior was preserved by its perimeter brick walls, regularly spaced paired and clerestory windows, and exposed metal roof trusses. By contrast, bold patterns, vivid colors, and curvaceous forms make a spirited statement about student life, adding elements of surprise and vigor within the building's staid envelope.

Upon entering one is greeted by: a 90-foot diameter linoleum rendition of the college

2

A   MAILBOXES
B   CONVENIENCE
     STORE
C   PUB
D   KITCHEN
E   STUDENT
     ORGANIZATIONS
F   CONFERENCE
G   INFORMATION
H   CAMPUS OFFICE
I   COPY CENTER
J   CAMPUS OFFICE

3

5

6

7

seal on the lounge floor, its student-designed stencils of floral patterns and polar bear mascot painted upon skewed walls, and the perforated-metal light fixtures, along the ramp that connects all activities. As it spirals up the union's two-tiered plan, the ramp's undulating form harks back to the Bowdoin pines, another college symbol. Most program elements are housed within colorful, flakeboard boxes just beyond the ramp.

Residual spaces become intimate places for study, conversation, and eating. Careful modulation of size and scale allows the building comfortably to accommodate solitary activities, small group meetings, and campus-wide social events. From vantage points along its balconies, the building permits glimpses of the activities within and the campus beyond.

The college has described the building as a "textbook student union," doing precisely what student unions are meant to do but rarely achieve.

5. *Custom light fixture detail*
6. *Custom clock*
7. *Existing condition*
8. *Interior with processional ramp*

NEW VICTORY THEATER

New York, New York, 1995

1. Existing exterior, 1992
2. Orchestra level plan
3. Restored façade along 42nd Street

74 When it opened in 1900, the New Victory, then named Hammerstein's Theatre Republic, was the first theater on the legendary block between Broadway and Eighth Avenue. In 1931 it became the city's first home of the striptease, and later the street's first pornographic movie theater. Its restoration was the first undertaken by The New 42nd Street to demonstrate that change was possible on the block, which helped to define its responsibility to the historic theaters as part of a partnership of public and private organizations committed to the redevelopment of 42nd Street. The building's transformation from an abandoned landmark to the city's first non-profit performing arts institution dedicated to year-round programming for young audiences was a milestone in the renaissance of popular entertainment in the historic theater district.

This building, the city's oldest surviving theater, resonates with a distinguished and multilayered history. Designed by Albert E. Westover and built for the producer Oscar Hammerstein, the "Father of Times Square," its elaborately decorated interior, featuring a large, gilded dome with plaster angels perched on its rim, wowed critics. Two years after its opening, the theater was renamed for the new owner, the impresario David Belasco, who executed a major interior renovation. The Victory reverted to its original name in 1914, when Belasco left to build a new Belasco Theater. Two more decades passed before the burlesque producer Billy Minsky added his name to the building, which was again renamed in 1942 the Victory. The theater played host to such legendary performers as Lillian Gish, Houdini, Claudette Colbert, and John and Lionel Barrymore and was home to such shows as *Abie's Irish Rose.*

The Victory is a miniature opera house, unlike any theater extant in the city. The intricacy of delicate interior details and numerous modifications over time mandated an existing-conditions report from which it was possible to create a master plan for restoration and rehabilitation. Because each of the theater's owners had added decorative elements and eliminated others, an interpretive, rather than a restoration approach, was chosen, which would make it

1

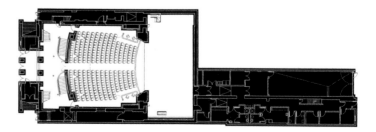

2

15   30   60

4

5

a viable, contemporary place. Its complex history is honored with the restoration of all existing elements of Hammerstein's façade and Belasco's interior. New public spaces deliberately separate the two.

On the exterior the grand double stair has been recreated, complete with ornate, standing globe lamps. Inside, the site's size limited the number of amenities audiences have come to expect in performance venues. To create a new public lobby on the main floor, the auditorium was reduced from 700 to 500 seats. New lobby, restroom, and concession spaces were literally carved out of solid rock in the basement level. Of the two buildings behind the theater, one was razed to make way for a new loading dock; the other converted to dressing rooms and support space. A new elevator for disabled access, HVAC systems, and sophisticated theater equipment were unobtrusively added to meet contemporary needs.

Within the auditorium, detailed plaster and woodwork were meticulously restored. Cast plaster angels once again embrace their lyres and surround the freshly stippled, blue ceiling dome. Elaborate stacked boxes on either side of the stage, faux plaster draperies, and gilded plasterwork including fleur-de-lis, laurel wreaths, and winged female figures were repaired and refinished. The custom-designed carpeting and upholstery are accented with the theater's deep reds, gold, and touches of purple and green. Wrought iron stanchions and new seats are patterned with the same bumblebee motif used in the original plasterwork, to honor Belasco.

The integration of new and clearly modern public and support spaces between exterior and interior layers of history contributes to the Victory's evolution. It also inspires admiration for the larger revitalization of 42nd Street and a rejuvenated commitment to public life in New York.

4. View from the stage
5. Detail of new lobby stairs
6. View of auditorium from upper balcony

AMERICAN INDIAN WING

**New York State Historical Association
Fenimore House
Cooperstown, New York, 1995**

Since 1945 the New York State Historical Association has been located in a former residence built by Edward Severin Clark, on lakeside property once owned by James Fenimore Cooper. In 1992 the association, a private educational institution dedicated to the study of New York State and American history and culture, was given by Eugene and Clare Thaw, an impressive collection of more than 700 Native American artifacts. The art collectors gathered these works, dating from precontact times to the late twentieth century, from across the nation. Considered one of the most important private collections of its kind assembled in the last fifty years, it needed an ideal setting for exhibition and conservation.

Jane Forbes Clark, Edward's niece, donated an 18,000-square-foot addition to the 1932 neo-Georgian house to exhibit the Thaw collection. HHPA's design responded to Clark's desire that modifications to the mansion remain discreet and celebrate the beauty of its landscape. HHPA therefore chose to locate the new galleries so that their roof provides support for a garden terrace whose levels, pavilions, and plantings provide a handsome overlook to the 8-mile Lake Otsego. A new underground service passage links the museum to the adjacent library and research center. As a result, it was possible to remove a second paved service entry, which prohibited the landscape from fully embracing the house.

In addition to conserving the rolling lawns that sweep down to the lakeshore, HHPA sought a design appropriate to a contemporary museum, one that would not upstage or endanger its collection. In order to preserve the many fragile, light-sensitive objects, the new wing meets the highest standards of museum conservation. Systems that maintain stable temperature and humidity shield all objects from contamination and atmospheric change. Further precautionary measures include the use of specialized fiber optic lighting systems and construction materials with acceptable off-gassing characteristics.

When visitors arrive at Fenimore House, they enter through an imposing neo-Georgian portico into a small vestibule. Before them a new, grand double stair

1. Rooftop terrace view of Fenimore House
2. Terrace pavilion view
3. Terrace view toward Lake Otsego
4. Overleaf: American Indian Wing at night

1, 2

3

4

5

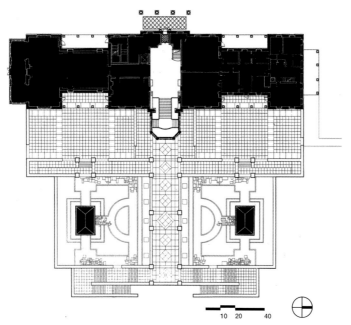

6

descends to the central exhibition hall below. This stately room, supported by ten columns of solid Casota stone each weighing more than two tons, offers access to two galleries, a 121-seat auditorium, a study center, storage areas, and support facilities. Because the site slopes down, the hall also offers magnificent, unexpected views of the lake and surrounding hills.

The main hall showcases some of the collection's larger works. Flanking it are two galleries with exhibitions designed by Stephen Saitas. One houses a permanent installation; the other is devoted to rotating shows. A simple, abstract interior vocabulary forms a background for display. The materials are warm: yellow-beige stone columns and floors, natural-finish maple ceilings and casework, and yellow-beige carpet and paint colors, accented with white.

Artifacts not displayed in galleries can be viewed in glass-fronted cabinets in the study center, an open storage area and classroom facility. This is an important resource for visiting scholars and students of the Cooperstown Graduate Program in History Museum Studies.

The new American Indian Wing complements the architecture of the Fenimore House, becoming a picturesque extension of the landscape. The progression from one to the other expresses the continuity of time and place special to Cooperstown.

4. Main hall
5. Grand double stair
6. Entry level plan
7. Entrance to Thaw Collection from main hall
8. Overleaf: American Indian Wing at night

10   20   40

The Eugene and Clare Thaw Gallery

TEMPLE ISRAEL

Dayton, Ohio, 1995

84

Since its formation in 1850, Congregation Temple Israel has been housed in five buildings — a converted bank, a former Baptist church, a synagogue, an Albert Kahn building, and now a new building, dedicated in 1995. As the number of congregation members declined, the temple leaders felt a more intimate space in a central location would draw attendance from the suburban communities straddled by Dayton, as well as from the immediate downtown area.

Situated in Riverside Park, a picturesque, 12-acre green space along the Great Miami River, the new building boasts a spectacular view of the downtown skyline. In a long-term agreement with the city, the congregation was granted 3 acres for its new home in exchange for developing and maintaining the park's other 9 acres.

In commissioning a new synagogue, the 800-member congregation directed only that it be rooted in the tradition of synagogue architecture, which is ageless and dignified. Their principal requirements were programmatic.

Religious buildings have traditionally fulfilled a multitude of needs. They are places for worship, education, life-cycle ceremonies, holiday observances, cultural events, and social gatherings. Their use and enjoyment by people of all ages makes flexibility a key factor in their design. Temple Israel houses a sanctuary, a great hall, a chapel, classrooms, a library, a gift shop, a kitchen, and other educational and administrative

1. Site plan
2. South façade
3. Great Miami River passing Temple Israel and downtown Dayton

2, 3

1

100 200 300

4

5

spaces. The convergence of rooms, each with a distinct geometry, results in a series of connected chambers and passageways that function as an active lobby space.

Within the plan of closely related rooms, the sanctuary is its fulcrum. In order to create an intimate space for 320 worshippers, or a fraction of that number, the sanctuary is composed of a central pentagon with fixed seating for 200. Loose seating for another 120 is provided atop platforms along its square perimeter. The room is oriented east, toward Jerusalem, and defined by four structural clay-tile walls. Five Douglas fir columns incline inward to frame a polyhedral skylight and to support a wooden plank ceiling and metal shingle roof. Sunlight filters down through a reflector to the congregation and bimah. At its center, three receding poplar-wood planes culminate in an ark screen, created by artist Albert Paley. The earth-inspired aesthetic of timber and clay is reinforced by green, vine-patterned upholstery and a leaf-patterned carpet.

Adjacent to the sanctuary, the great hall accommodates 800 for services, 350 for banquets, or can be partitioned to create three smaller rooms. Its east wall and roof follow a cosine curve, which underscores the importance of the ark and bimah, placed at its deepest point. From the exterior, the undulating wall responds to the gentle flow and bends of the river it faces.

The chapel is linked to the temple's recent past. The ark, screen wall, eternal light, and stained-glass windows from the previous temple have been integrated with a new walnut- and cherry-paneled room with views to the surrounding park. An interior courtyard separates the sacred spaces from the twelve classrooms that encase an L-shaped corridor.

Temple Israel is a contemporary manifestation of 3000 years of Judaic tradition. Its underlying, subtle allusions to the design of previous Hebrew sanctuaries and to the continuity of religious ceremony strengthen its ties to synagogues of every era.

4. Great hall
5. Lobby
6. Floor plan
7. Skylight detail in sanctuary
8. Overleaf: Riverside at night

1 SANCTUARY
2 GREAT HALL
3 CHAPEL
4 LOBBY
5 ADMINISTRATION
6 EDUCATION
7 KITCHEN
8 COURTYARD

6

10 20   40

9. Sanctuary with Albert Paley ark screen
10. Chapel with reused ark and stained glass

10

LIED EDUCATION
CENTER FOR THE ARTS

Creighton University
Omaha, Nebraska, 1996

92 Creighton University's fine and performing arts departments, previously scattered across campus in adapted spaces, have been consolidated in the Lied Education Center for the Arts. In its plan and forms the building symbolizes the diversity and vitality of these activities and attests to the university's commitment to education and artistic development.

Prior to winning a design competition for the center, HHPA had been asked by the university to prepare a program for it. As the first permanent home for the arts, the building takes advantage of the visibility of its site at the intersection of a major vehicular thoroughfare and the main campus walkway to give the arts a prominent identity.

The center is a stepped cube of stone, buff brick, exposed concrete, and glass curtain wall. These materials, which were previously used elsewhere on campus, are combined here to signify the unification of the university's arts programs. Rising out of the cube at various points are five pentagonal towers of tan-speckled limestone, mined from an ancient seabed, with visible fish fossil imprints. Three floor levels, terraced into the sloping site, house an art gallery and flexible performance and teaching spaces for drama, dance, music, painting, life drawing, sculpture, ceramics, printmaking, art history, and photography.

At the physical and programmatic heart of the building is a 350-seat, one-balcony proscenium theater with an orchestra pit capable of rising three-levels. Its stage tower, the largest in Omaha, accommodates a variety of production and presentation types. Complementing the performance space are dressing rooms, costume, scene, and prop shops, and a green room. It is surrounded by a variety of theater, music, and dance studios and practice rooms.

Vertically connected residual space on the lowest and middle levels creates a two-story lobby for receptions and pre- and post-performance use. The lobby's east side consists of an aluminum-and-glass curtain wall, with ceramic frit reducing the amount

1. Main entrance

2

3

of direct sunlight. Interior partitions of clay tile, exposed concrete, drywall, brick, ribbed ceramic tile, and glass enliven the environment. Exposed ductwork, light fixtures, and air-handling ducts add drama to this space and contrast with vibrantly colored fabrics and finishes, such as Persian-style printed carpeting, cherry-wood panels, and green and red-clay tile.

This mix of materials enabled HHPA to concentrate the project's resources on commodious and technologically sophisticated performance and teaching spaces. The 71,600-square-foot structure was built for less than $140 per square foot. With its variegated exterior profile and bold interior palette visible through the curtain wall, it radiates creative energy along an otherwise serene walkway.

2. Rooftop detail
3. Limestone and brick patterning
4. First floor plan
5. Façade detail

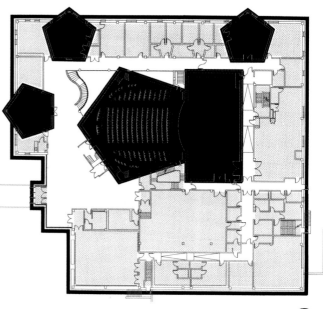

4

10 20   40

7

8

6. Auditorium
7. Lobby stairwell
8. Stair entry to auditorium

9

10

9. Art gallery
10. Printmaking shop
11. Sculpture studio

EXXON SERVICE STATION

Orlando, Florida, 1996

100   Commissioned by the Disney Development Company, HHPA's design for the Exxon Service Station, at the main entrance to the Epcot Hotels complex, responds to Florida's regional landscape and a pivotal location. The 1.3-acre site was conceived as a tropical island, with bungalow-like architecture and a ring of palm trees encircled by water.

Taking full advantage of Florida's mild climate, HHPA sheltered the eight pumps and the service building with a canopy of gabled trelliswork, creating the feel of an open garden pavilion. The trellises, varying in width and pattern, are superimposed, entangling the sun's rays and creating a shifting matrix of shadows.

Nestled below the steel armature of the canopy is a 2000-square-foot service building. The structure's vibrant colors, metal-louvered glass curtain wall, and hipped blue corrugated-metal roof are reminiscent of a Caribbean hut, offering shade while remaining open to the environment. At night the station is theatrically lit by thousand-watt quartz uplights. Day or night the openwork profile of the station and its enticing parklike setting attract attention from a distance across Florida's predominantly flat landscape. Devoid of the towering signs associated with most roadway architecture, the station has established its own identity as an appropriate gateway into Walt Disney World Resort.

Commonplace materials and tropical landscaping elements were used to achieve dramatic effects, giving the station high visibility while responding to the lush, sun-drenched setting in which it resides.

1. Station at dusk
2. Site plan
3. Alternative scheme model
4. Alternative scheme model

1

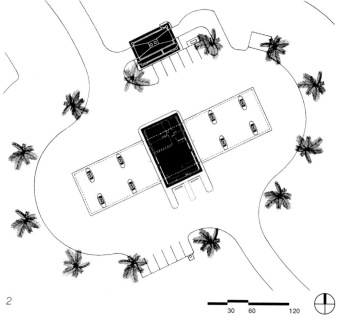

2

30   60   120

3

4

HAWAII THEATRE CENTER

Honolulu, Hawaii, 1996

102   Similar to many communities seeking to revitalize their downtown, restoration of the Hawaii Theatre was considered pivotal to the renaissance of Oahu's historic Chinatown district. Proclaimed the Pride of the Pacific when it opened in 1922, the theater was a popular showplace for vaudeville, plays, and musicals. Following World War II it became a swank movie palace. As the entertainment scene gradually shifted from downtown to Waikiki and the island's suburbs, the theater struggled financially and ultimately closed in 1984.

A small group of concerned citizens organized to save the theater, which is listed on the national and state registers of historic places. Mary Bishop, who had spearheaded a community effort resulting in the salvation of the historic Ohio Theatre in Columbus, was brought in to evaluate the building. Her first recommendation was to ask HHPA, who modernized and expanded the Ohio Theatre (1984), to gauge the efforts required to rescue the Hawaii Theatre and make it a viable enterprise. Outwardly it seemed to be in good shape, but its interior had been almost entirely ravaged by termites. Though structurally deficient, the auditorium offered an unusually intimate seating configuration, and all agreed it was worth saving.

Over the next ten years, the theater accumulated, from public and private sources, funding sufficient to develop a master plan, to secure expansion capabilities by acquiring portions of the city block on which the theater sits, and to finance phase-one improvements. To draw

2

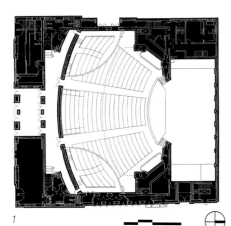
1   10   20   40

3

5

10

6

7

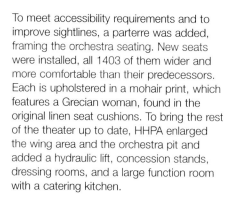

8

9

audiences from all segments of the community, HTC established acoustical and architectural excellence as its design standard. New sound, lighting, and projection systems were carefully integrated, and its proscenium mural, The Glorification of Drama, by Lionel Walden, was restored, as were its many Shakespearean motif trompe l'oeil mosaics and bas-reliefs.

To meet accessibility requirements and to improve sightlines, a parterre was added, framing the orchestra seating. New seats were installed, all 1403 of them wider and more comfortable than their predecessors. Each is upholstered in a mohair print, which features a Grecian woman, found in the original linen seat cushions. To bring the rest of the theater up to date, HHPA enlarged the wing area and the orchestra pit and added a hydraulic lift, concession stands, dressing rooms, and a large function room with a catering kitchen.

Future phases will include the exterior restoration of the theater, expansion of the stage, and a new four-story pavilion adjacent to it, accommodating an expanded lobby, support and backstage facilities, new offices, and arts-related commercial and retail spaces.

In the two years since reopening in April 1996, the theater has been tremendously successful, filling an important and unique niche by producing a variety of performing arts activities for mid-size audiences, which have drawn more than 500,000 patrons.

---

5. *View of stage from balcony*
6. *View of box seats from under balcony*
7. *Box seats*
8. *View looking up from box seats*
9. *Trompe l'oeil mosaic*
10. *Two-thirds of "The Glorification of the Drama" mural by Lionel Walden, 1990*
11. *View from under balcony*

MULTNOMAH COUNTY CENTRAL LIBRARY

Portland, Oregon, 1997

1. Restored exterior
2. First floor plan
3. Starbucks café in popular library
4. Information desk

106 When the library opened in 1913, it was considered one of the most modern in the nation. The collaboration of Portland architect Albert E. Doyle and library chief Mary Frances Isom resulted in a highly efficient Georgian revival building with a series of large, open rooms surrounding a central monumental stair and a tower of stacks. Its straightforward organization facilitated the management of large numbers of people, and made for easy interaction between patrons and librarians. In 1994 when it closed for renovation, it served the largest number of patrons per square foot of any public library in the nation.

In the years prior to its rehabilitation, the library suffered from overcrowding; environmental, security, and telecommunications needs went unfulfilled; and electrical failures were commonplace. More than 70 percent of the collection was housed in closed, cast-iron stacks. Wheelchair access was difficult if not impossible in some areas. Most significantly, the building's unreinforced masonry walls required considerable seismic strengthening.

HHPA's renovation and expansion of the 123,600-square-foot building, in association with Portland architects Fletcher Farr Ayotte, revitalizes a well-loved landmark. Listed on the National Register of Historic Places, the library's meticulously restored brick and limestone façade confirms a strong civic presence. The original windows and delicate wooden mullions were retained to preserve the exterior appearance.

1

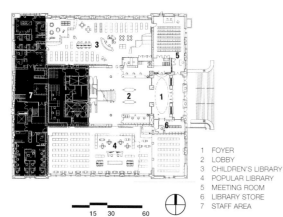

1 FOYER
2 LOBBY
3 CHILDREN'S LIBRARY
4 POPULAR LIBRARY
5 MEETING ROOM
6 LIBRARY STORE
7 STAFF AREA

15 30 60

2

3

Inside, the building was replanned to accommodate contemporary library services, including greater access to materials, integration of state-of-the-art technologies, and expanded community facilities. At ground level, a new series of vestibules and lobby spaces gives direct access to a multipurpose meeting room, library store, and a new "welcome" desk for tour groups. Much of the first floor is now devoted to public use, with a significantly enlarged children's room that features a new story theater, and an expanded popular library that entices visitors with a Starbucks coffee bar and current best sellers.

Following the strong organization of the original design, reading rooms are situated along three sides of the library, with new support areas along the fourth. A discreet two-story roof addition accommodates administrative offices.

The work of the artist Larry Kirkland graces the interior design, which is based on the library's theme, "A Garden of Knowledge." Interwoven organic motifs become a point of discovery, leading visitors into the heart of the library. Custom carpets, wallpaper, and pendant light fixtures are patterned with leaves and roses, the flower of Portland. In the children's library, a bronze tree by the artists Dana Lynn Louis and Barbara Eiswerth sprouts sculpted symbols of children's literature and learning.

The public spaces on each floor are distinguished by pastel colors accented with white ceilings and window trim in true Georgian style. Custom tables, for the more than 130 public computers, conceal telecommunications lines and wires and allow users to plug in personal laptops. Technology is respectfully integrated within the stately rooms, while insuring flexibility to adapt to change.

In addition to seismically strengthening a beloved civic landmark, the restored library now offers greater access to its collections, easier check-out and return services, on-line catalogues and networked databases, and new amenities, from snacking and shopping to musical performances. The spirit of collaboration that gave the original its strong "bones" — efficient organization and light-filled interiors — was continued eighty years later, when the library was returned to its community, newly equipped for the twenty-first century.

5

6

5. Children's room with Tree of Knowledge sculpture by artists Dana Lynn Louis and Barbara Eiswerth
6. Granite stairs engraved with leaf and floral patterns by artist Larry Kirkland
7. Restored reading room

WINDOWS ON THE WORLD

New York, New York, 1996

1. 107th floor plan
2. 106th floor plan
3. Restaurant with view north

110 Occupying two acres of space on the 106th and 107th floors of the World Trade Center, Tower One, Windows on the World is an internationally renowned restaurant. Following the 1993 terrorist bombing that damaged the building, its owner, the Port Authority of New York and New Jersey, was determined to reconstruct the restaurant and uphold its tradition as a place of sophisticated cuisine, great vistas, and contemporary design.

The restaurant's operator, the Joseph Baum & Michael Whiteman Company, also HHPA's client for restoration of the Rainbow Room (1987), wanted Windows on the World to open in June 1996. This translated into twenty-three months for design and construction of 80,000 square feet of user-intensive space.

Fine dining environments traditionally employ a classic decor to create an aura of elegance. Windows on the World is a departure. No historical references guided the design of the restaurant's fifteen enclosures, and no two are the same. The design's precedent lies in the city itself, its constantly changing and diverse panorama. Every design consideration enhances both the feeling of being more than one thousand feet in the air and the experience of gazing upon the cityscape from numerous vantage points. These views, like no other in the world, are complemented by distinctive interior schemes.

The original restaurant, which opened in 1976, included careful platforming of tables to maximize views, but spaces and finishes were uniform and wheelchair access impossible. The renovation heightens the dining environment with a broader spectrum of materials, manipulation of floor slope, and finishes that contrast hard reflective surfaces with soft, luxurious ones.

Views from Windows on the World are breathtaking, not only because of altitude, but also because of light and shadow. Every day brings changes of color, direction, and intensity of the sun, together with cloud movements and atmospheric conditions. The drama of the natural landscape, night and day, is complemented by the restaurant's design, which acknowledges distant horizons, city profiles at long-range, and more immediate street grids alike, from all points on the compass.

When views are nonexistent on foggy or rainy days, the architectural character of each room asserts itself as a surrogate for the thrill of looking outward. In the arrival gallery on the 107th floor, for example, curved walls of striped fabric join a curtain of glistening, undulating glass beads, designed by Milton Glaser, in an abstract pattern of clouds and sky. A terrazzo floor simulates Mercator's projection of the globe, with five arcs ranging in tone, divided by strips of zinc inset with fiber optics. The promenade to the Greatest Bar on Earth, the Skybox, private dining suites, and Windows on the World Restaurant features a custom-woven carpet depicting sixteen international city grids. On the 106th floor, guests are greeted in a welcoming area whose carpet recalls the colors of lower Manhattan at twilight.

A terrazzo surface, patterned after Piazza San Marco in Venice, defines the three-bar area at the Greatest Bar on Earth. As the floor slopes down from the door to the windows, the ceiling steps up almost two feet, opening the room to views beyond. Four blown-glass skyscrapers by the artist Dan Dailey are illuminated from within, blurring the distinction between interior and exterior.

HHPA enhanced the basic configuration of the restaurant, used sensuous, softer finishes, and added four origami-style ceilings over special seating areas for greater intimacy. At Cellar in the Sky, the marble floor was raised to align flush bottom with its windows so the room appears to hover above New York harbor. Both the Liberty and Hudson Suites were equipped with operable wall enclosures for utmost flexibility. All of these efforts were made to achieve a contemporary setting for dining, entertainment, and private occasions. Windows on the World's new interior decor is a reflection of the vast and diverse cityscape far below. It encourages the public to return and rediscover the city.

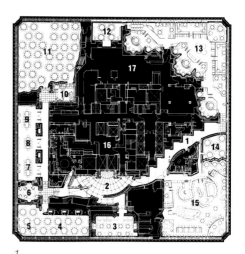

1

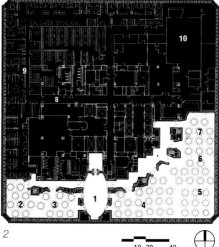

2

10 20   40

4

5

4. Mirrored planes on the 106th floor
5. Entry to the 106th floor
6. Cellar in the Sky

7

8

7. *The Greatest Bar on Earth*
8. *Carpet patterns combine street grids
of sixteen cities*
9. *The Greatest Bar on Earth (with four
hand-blown "skyscrapers" by artist Dan Daily)*

488 MADISON AVENUE

New York, New York, 1997

116 In 1949 Emery Roth & Sons completed the construction of the twenty-three-story office building that occupies a full block on the west side of Madison Avenue between 51st and 52nd streets. Later known as the Look Building, after one of its major tenants, *Look* magazine, the structure was a forerunner to the hundreds of International Style buildings that were to grace New York City in later decades. What continues to distinguish 488 Madison from the ubiquitous postwar architecture of midtown is its purely horizontal emphasis and it's curved corners. The building rises in a series of asymmetrical setbacks with rounded corners and strip windows. The visibility of vertical columns is diminished behind alternating horizontal bands of steel-framed glass and white brick.

Nearly half a century later, renovation and restoration were required to preserve this significant example of American modernism. HHPA's mission was to make the building environmentally sound and viable for contemporary business use and to return it to its original appearance. The exterior of the building has been cleaned and repainted. Deteriorated glazed bricks and copings were replaced, as were the roof and paved terraces on upper floors. Original single-glazed, steel-frame windows were replaced with new, operable, aluminum, double-glazed windows. Though prohibitive costs forced the decision to use aluminum instead of steel, making the frames larger, the existing mullion and operable window patterns were retained. An extruded vertical fin at each window juncture invigorates the façade with reflected light and shadow.

Dramatic improvements make the lobby more hospitable. Its shape has been refined, in a manner sympathetic to the original, to enhance circulation and identity. A new 5-foot exterior canopy complements this redefinition. Entrance walls, previously a stark white marble, are now clad in a warmer pink and yellow Minnesota stone with bands of black terrazzo. The two-tone granite floors are laid in a 1950s striped pattern. On the upper levels, the tenant lobbies have been redesigned in a similar fashion to lend consistency to the building's appearance.

1

Throughout 488 Madison's history, the lobby has undergone various modernizations to meet the changing expectations of its tenants. As part of current upgrades, a concierge desk and newsstand were located within existing recesses of the lobby to preserve its design intent. The lighting was also redesigned to eliminate harsh downlighting and inappropriate fixture additions. New light fixtures extend from wall to wall to create the illusion of a lobby twice its width. All of the building's nine elevators have been refurbished. The interior of each cab features a new stone skin that repeats the pattern of the lobby walls.

The process of restoring modernist buildings is unlike that of turn-of-the-century buildings. Rather than preserve original features in an attempt to reveal the passage of time, the inherent nature of modernism calls for replacement of elements to return appearances to a crisp minimalism. Today 488 Madison shimmers in the streetscape. Its clean exterior surface and new metallic fins demand the same attention as new buildings.

1. *Curved window detail with new vertical fin*
2. *Street level plan*
3. *Partial Madison Avenue east façade*

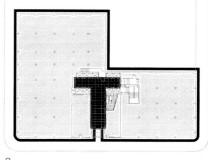

2

15 30   60

NEW AMSTERDAM THEATRE

New York, New York, 1997

118 The New Amsterdam, designed by Henry Herts and Hugh Tallant in 1903, is as celebrated for its architectural exuberance and technical achievement as it is for the performers who graced its stage. It is perhaps most well known as the home of the Ziegfeld Follies from 1913 until 1927. In 1937 it became a movie house and gained a new streamlined marquee and entry. Subsequent alterations occurred, the most dramatic in 1953, when twelve of the auditorium's seating boxes were destroyed to make way for a wide CinemaScope movie screen. After a spiraling decline that mirrored the demise of Times Square, the theater's presentation of second-run movies ended in 1982. The property was bought but then abandoned. For ten years it sat partially exposed to the weather, suffering decay and water damage.

As part of a plan to revitalize the historic 42nd Street theater district, New York State purchased the property in 1992, and the 42nd Street Development Project commissioned HHPA to make recommendations for the theater's renewal and find ways to stabilize it until developers could be located to buy, lease, or restore it. One year later, Michael Eisner, the Chairman and CEO of The Walt Disney Company, toured the dilapidated building. Despite puddles of water, mushrooms growing from the orchestra floor, and birds flying overhead, Eisner was quick to recognize the romance and latent splendor of the space. Before the year's end a lease was signed.

HHPA's challenge was to determine how best to re-create the landmark theater's magnificent decorative scheme. To bring the theater back to its original 1903 condition would require wholesale replacement of its murals and woodwork. Instead, HHPA's objective was an "interpretive restoration," creating a seamless whole that would both acknowledge the passage of time but allow it to become a dazzling contemporary venue for live Disney productions.

The theater's appalling condition made restoration a daunting undertaking. None of the original decorative scheme remained intact. A combination of paint analyses and historical documentation by Building

1

2

3

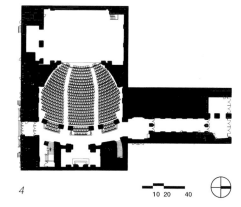

4

10 20 40

1. Theater circa 1907
2. Theater circa 1925
3. Section through auditorium
4. Orchestra level plan
5. Restored marquee on 42nd Street

6

7

8

9

Conservation Associates helped to restore elements that had been removed, painted over, or obscured. Special painting and glazing techniques insured that these sections would not look too new after restoration. Modern technology enabled custom computer-generated designs of carpeting, seat coverings, and stage curtains whose colors and textures were in keeping with the theater's original decorative spirit.

The theater's eclectic mix of exuberant ornament includes plaster relief panels of scenes from Shakespeare and Wagner, elaborate murals of "Creation" and "Inspiration," terracotta relief panels depicting themes like "Progress," balustrades with monkeys and squirrels, and an abundance of the floral and foliate representations that characterized the Art Nouveau decoration. A proscenium arch, ornamented with sixteen plaster peacocks entwined with vines and flanked by murals of "Virtue" and "Courage," has been restored to dramatic effect. The twelve boxes, each named for a different flower, have been totally reconstructed to again embrace the stage.

Amenities, including air conditioning, expanded lobby space on the mezzanine and balcony levels, commodious men's and women's lounges, and elevator access to the balconies have all been introduced to the building. State-of-the-art stage lighting, rigging, sound systems are unobtrusively inserted. Seating capacity is expanded from 1750 to 1814 seats.

In addition to its luxurious decor and technical enhancements, the New Amsterdam boasts the fourth largest stage in New York, and four large public spaces, such as the voluptuous, elliptical New Amsterdam Room, the vaulted Grand Foyer, and the oak-paneled General Reception Room.

Now fully restored, the New Amsterdam's rich history and splendid interior make it a pinnacle of 42nd Street's transformation. Like the Times Square renewal itself, our interpretive design celebrates the spirit of place, restoring a beloved theater into a showplace.

6. The New Amsterdam Room, 1994
7. The New Amsterdam Room restored
8. The Grand Foyer restored
9. Auditorium, 1994
10. Auditorium restored

11

12

13

14

15

16

17

18

19

20

11. Detail of wood paneling
12. Elliptical domed ceiling
13. Reconstructed boxes
14. Detail of elevator door
15. The New Amsterdam Room
16. Refurbished figures atop the auditorium dome
17. One of four plaster peacocks
18. View of box seating from balcony
19. Relief of "Progress" below stained glass skylight
20. Terra-cotta monkey on banister

SALISBURY UPPER SCHOOL

Salisbury, Maryland, 1997

1. Detail of corrugated steel arches
2. First floor plan
3. Site plan
4. Main entrance
5. North façade

124　In 1972 HHPA designed the Salisbury Lower School, a progressive learning institution for prekindergarten to eighth grade students. Its imaginative composition and open plan supported the school's mission by stimulating curiosity, allowing children to explore different subject areas, and advance academically and socially at their own rate.

The success of the independent elementary school led to the need, twenty-five years later, for a new upper school for grades nine through twelve. The client wanted the facility to have the same qualities as the lower school. In their description of the project, they asked for open, airy spaces connected to the outdoors with unusual window placements, use of natural light, flexible, efficient use of space, and less expensive, low-maintenance building systems and finishes.

A 26-acre site west of the original school had been donated for the new facilities, which included a gymnasium as well as classrooms. The contours of the open field slope gently and contrast dramatically with the thickly wooded setting of the existing school.

Several similarities exist between the two generations of buildings. Like the original, a one-story box bisected by a triangular tunnel, geometrically shaped windows punctuate the upper school's volumes. Interior plans in both feature partitions, set on rotated axes, that define open and closed areas for a variety of teaching situations, and amorphous residual spaces for less structured encounters. Brightly colored beams, columns, and railings, vigorously patterned carpets, and skylights intensify both learning environments.

At the center of the upper school is a conical domed structure that encloses the library, administrative offices, and informal gathering spaces. From this hub radiate a landscaped vehicular drop-off area, an academic wing, an athletic wing, and, on the fourth axis, space for a future expansion.

Eight teaching spaces, of varying heights and degrees of enclosure, are located along the periphery of the academic wing. Glass-partitioned faculty offices are dispersed

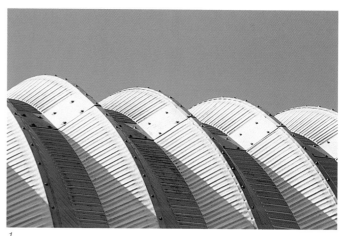

1

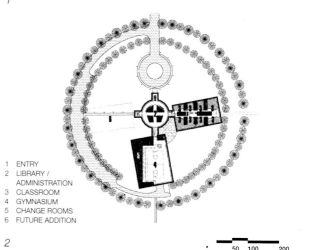

1　ENTRY
2　LIBRARY /
　　ADMINISTRATION
3　CLASSROOM
4　GYMNASIUM
5　CHANGE ROOMS
6　FUTURE ADDITION

2

50　100　　200

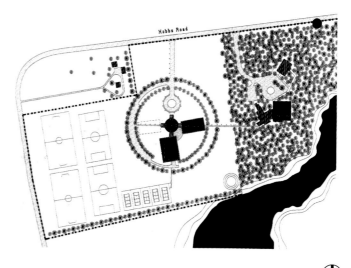

3

125　250　　　500

4, 5

6

9

among classrooms; their visibility furthers the school's sense of community. In the athletic wing, an open gymnasium, surrounded by support spaces, is set on angle within the larger, rectangular volume.

The building's budget, $95 per square foot, was established by escalating the unit cost of the original building to 1997 dollars. Achieving a building of character with such modest means meant applying ingenuity in using inexpensive materials in innovative ways. A prefabricated storage dome with octagonal windows was purchased for the hub and connects to vinyl-sided wings through corrugated steel arches. Customized features, such as exterior copper cladding, interior wood finishing, and a colored-glass cupola offset its standard roadside appearance. Coupled with limited resources, a tight schedule led to employing a design-build process. The upper school welcomed its first class of students a little more than eighteen months after HHPA was commissioned.

6. Library
7. Connecting corridor
8. Administrative cluster
9. View along periphery of dome
10. Open classrooms

7

8

THE SIENA

New York, New York, 1997

1. Entrance along 76th Street
2. Detail of door frieze
3. Site plan
4. View from 76th Street and Lexington Avenue

128   Creation of The Siena, a thirty-one-story residential building on Manhattan's Upper East Side, forms part of the restoration plan for St. Jean Baptiste Eglise, a National Register Landmark church. Income from the sale of the church's air rights insured funds critical to its restoration and maintenance program. Transfer of these air rights to an adjacent property made The Siena's construction possible.

The church was designed by Nicholas Serracino in the style of the Italian Renaissance. The Siena's design responds to the character of the church and its rectory as well as to the neighborhood's contemporary, high-rise apartment buildings. Commercial space in the lower portion of the building is clad in granite and cast stone to harmonize with the limestone and granite of the church's façade. Built to the street line, The Siena's base maintains the established streetwall and matches the church's cornice line, while the residential tower is set back along this line to acknowledge the church's volume.

The rich sculptural elements of the church cause a play of light and shadow that changes its appearance throughout the day. The Siena's angled niches form a continuation of these features. Horizontal belt courses correspond to the church cornices, and vertical facets set with windows allude to its two freestanding towers. Offsets and setbacks allow small design details, such as windows and turrets, to read clearly. The angled corners offer residents unexpected diagonal vistas of Manhattan. Balconies with wrought-iron railings further associate the building with the Upper East Side's residential character.

The Siena's mass, size, and articulation respond to its context, acknowledging the church and rectory whose landmark status made its construction possible, and place it prominently in the tradition of graceful, large-scale residential buildings for which New York City is celebrated.

1

2

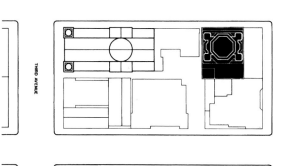

3

50   100   200

VILAR CENTER
FOR THE ARTS

Beaver Creek, Colorado, 1998

130   Beaver Creek is a mountain resort
       community in the Vail Valley of Colorado, a
       world-class ski destination that incorporates
       shops, restaurants, and luxury residences
       in a village environment. Its architectural
       character, developed over the past twenty
       years, is modeled on European alpine
       precedents. In 1995 as plans for the final
       phase of the core development in Beaver
       Creek were drawing to a close, HHPA was
       asked to design a multiuse theater under
       the village's new centerpiece — an ice rink.

       For many years the Vail Valley had sought
       to create a year-round counterpart to its
       outdoor summer performance venue, the
       Ford Amphitheater. The developers, East-
       West Partners, saw an opportunity on this
       site to build a true community arts center on
       the village's most valuable piece of property
       — as long as it was entirely underground.
       The site presented many challenges:
       limitations in size, an odd configuration of
       property lines, adjacent building pilings, poor
       geological conditions, and an underground
       stream. Each foot of excavation, needed
       to maximize the acoustical volume of the
       room, was measured in tens of thousands
       of dollars.

       Out of this, the new Vilar Center for the Arts,
       named for Alberto Vilar, its major donor, was
       created, with a classically inspired 530-seat
       theater, performance support spaces, public
       lobbies, and visual arts center.

       A sense of intimacy with a range of
       audience capacities was an important
       objective of the theater's design. The
       horseshoe seating arrangement, similar
       to those in many classic European halls,
       features a curved balcony and raised,
       parterre seating at orchestra level. This
       configuration draws the audience closer
       to the stage and insures excellent sightlines
       from each seat.

       Inspiration for the building's interiors was
       Colorado's majestic alpine environment. An
       autumnal palette of green, gold, amber, and
       rust captures the rich spectrum of colors
       found outdoors. Custom carpets and
       fabrics, whose aspen leaf patterns recall its

1. Theater view from balcony

mountainous setting, complement natural pinewood, used throughout the theater and public spaces. In the lobby these finishes are augmented by French limestone.

Because of the theater's subsurface location, much care was taken to isolate it acoustically from the rink and plaza. Acoustical-isolating springs in all walls and ceilings prevent the intrusion of noise from the skating and shopping above. Custom-designed velour acoustical curtains provide a range of acoustical environments and can be raised or lowered depending on the production. Utilization of variable acoustics affords the Beaver Creek Arts Foundation total flexibility in programming, enabling them to present a wide variety of performance types.

Though the rink does not permit a full-fly tower, a large side-stage area with full rigging is capable of handling a broad range of stage sets. Larger-than-usual stage wings were designed to accommodate the horizontal movement of scenery. Limited vertical space also dictated that lighting positions fall within the enclosure of the auditorium, rather than its attic. Lighting systems are supported by two bands of tension grids.

In addition to the theater, the Vilar Center includes a multilevel lobby and the May Gallery. The 2250-square-foot exhibition gallery doubles as a patrons' lounge during special performances and events. Direct access to the center is available from a covered vehicle drop-off at theater level, with escalator and elevator connections to the Village Plaza and ski slopes above.

The opening of the Vilar Center signals the cultural maturity of the Vail Valley. Renowned as premier ski territory, it is now also a first-rate arts destination. With fundraising led by former President Gerald Ford, honorary chair, the center was financed entirely with donations from the residents of Beaver Creek, who clearly believe that the arts are integral to the life of their community.

2. Lobby stairwell
3. Entry and balcony level plan
4. Orchestra level plan
5. Donor wall in lobby
6. Auditorium seating
7. May Gallery

2

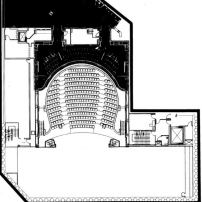

3

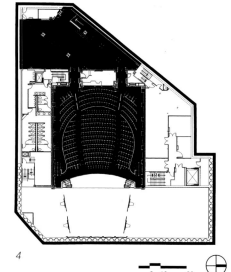

4

8 16   32

5, 6

7

BAMCAFÉ AND
BAM ROSE CINEMAS

Brooklyn Academy of Music
Brooklyn, New York, 1998

1. Brooklyn Academy of Music circa 1920s
2. BAMcafé viewed from balcony
3. BAMcafé

134 America's oldest performing arts center, Brooklyn Academy of Music (BAM), was a hub of social and cultural life after it opened in 1861. Since 1967 when Harvey Lichtenstein became executive producer, BAM has focused on contemporary artists and approaches to dance, theater, music, and opera. As the position BAM holds in the community has changed over the last century, so too have its programs.

HHPA's relationship with BAM developed along with the institution's renaissance. After a fire had destroyed the original BAM in 1903, Herts and Tallant, the premier theater architects of their day, designed a new neo-Italianate building to house a 2100-seat opera house, a 1400-seat music hall, a ballroom, lecture halls, offices, meeting rooms, and a 5000-square-foot lobby running the entire length of the building. Over the years the building was changed in an ad-hoc manner, rendering its circulation disjointed and confusing its patrons. In 1978 HHPA undertook an eight-phase renovation program that included the redesign and expansion of administrative, public, and support spaces in addition to a new rooftop rehearsal hall. In 1987 HHPA transformed the historic Majestic Theatre, two blocks away, into an award-winning 900-seat venue which opened with Peter Brook's adaptation of the Indian epic, *The Mahabharata*.

In 1994 BAM again asked HHPA to expand its public role and enhance its audience's experience, having become a leading showcase for the avant-garde and the cornerstone of a revitalization effort. New capital improvements not only provided needed patron amenities, but also completed the task of making BAM a unified architectural whole. A key component of this effort was conversion of the BAM Lepercq Space into the new BAMcafé.

This grand open space was once the ballroom and the heart of the BAM social scene. Its transformation restores its public purpose, serving a community that has a wide range of cultures and interests. Though located on the second floor, the BAMcafé functions as the primary lobby space, through the introduction of a new escalator. For those attending mainstage productions,

1

2

enhanced food and beverage service, new restrooms, and expanded pay-phone facilities are valued amenities. BAMcafé is also a destination for non–ticket holders who enjoy exchanging ideas in an engaging, informal environment.

Deep red openwork steel arches inset with corrugated, perforated metal recall the original decorative plaster vaults. The shimmering glow of silver-tipped light bulbs set along the arches accentuates their structure. Chairs, tables, lamps, and a stage platform can be rearranged (or removed) to accommodate a variety of activities including gala parties, live music performances, lectures and dialogues, and casual dining. At one end a refurbished balcony houses a control booth for lighting and sound; opposite, a new patron's lounge for intimate receptions looks over the BAMcafé. A new shop and portable retail stations allow patrons conveniently to purchase books, compact disks, and BAM souvenirs.

Amenities in the BAM ground floor entrance foyer have also been improved. Patron, press, and corporate sponsorship services have been consolidated. An openwork aluminum kiosk advertises upcoming events through printed collateral material and video monitors. New lighting enhances the architecture, illuminating the vaults and terrazzo floors. An exposed-brick wall lined with donor plaques is the backdrop for the new escalator.

The latest major initiative at BAM has involved reconfiguring the Helen Owen Carey Playhouse into a four-screen cinema. Two cinemas were created at street level and two at the mezzanine level. Screenings, in a variety of film formats, complement the work of artists who appear on BAM stages. A harmonious fusion of new and historic elements is announced in the concession area. Sleek refreshment stands are immersed between the intricately patterned arched entry vaults and elaborate wood detailing of the former inner lobby. Design of the cinemas unites the building's existing ornate plaster proscenium arch and coffered ceiling with contemporary cinema seating and state-of-the art sound and projection equipment.

Renewal of the BAM public spaces was achieved in a contemporary way, by juxtaposing new with old and, contrasting technological innovation with the ornate details of this historic building. These improvements are an essential part of a larger master plan, one that reinforces the BAM "campus" of arts and entertainment resources and dramatically increases the quality and intensity of its engagement with its community.

136

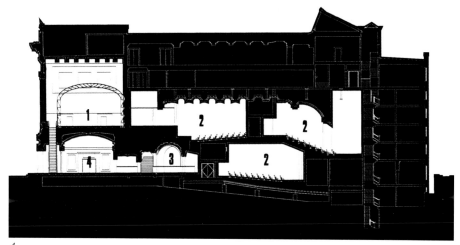

4. Section
5. Orchestra level plan
6. Concession area
7. Restored lobby with new escalator
8. Light fixture detail
9. Corridor leading to cinema

4

1 LEPERCQ SPACE
2 CINEMA
3 PROMENADE
4 MAIN LOBBY

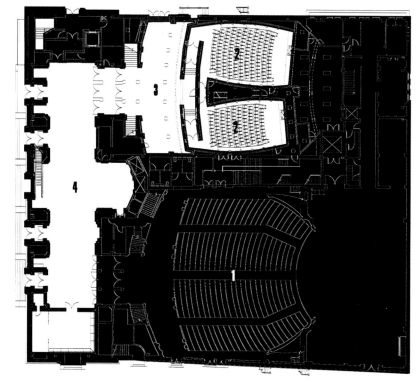

5

1 OPERA HOUSE
2 CINEMA
3 PROMENADE
4 MAIN LOBBY

10   20   40

6

7

8

9

10

10. Cinema #2, 156 seats
11. Cinema #4, 216 seats
12. Cinema #3, 300 seats
13. Cinema #3, view of seats

11

12

13

CLEVELAND PUBLIC LIBRARY

Cleveland, Ohio, 1998

1. Main entrance along Superior Avenue
2. Section through Main Library
and Louis Stokes Wing
3. Street level plan
4. View along Superior Avenue

140   HHPA's renovation and expansion of the Cleveland Public Library allowed it to enhance and augment services. The new Louis Stokes Wing, which accommodates additional library materials, state-of-the-art technology, and an auditorium enlarges the main library by some 255,000 square feet, nearly doubling its size. The old and new buildings, which connect underground, are separated at grade by the Eastman Reading Garden, an intimate park that is one of the most beloved green spaces in downtown Cleveland.

The Main Library Renovation

The library, which had originally opened in 1869 in modest rented quarters, opened at its current location, at 325 Superior Avenue, in 1925. The main library building was designed in the neoclassical style by Walker and Weeks, and adhered to the principles of the Cleveland Group Plan, a visionary document developed by Burnham, Brunner, and Carrere in 1903. The plan's implementation over subsequent decades resulted in a harmonious ensemble of beaux-arts civic buildings that surround a ceremonial mall facing Lake Erie, whose south terminus is formed by the library and the adjoining Federal Building, of uniform height, width, and massing.

HHPA's restoration of the main library includes the retention of important historic elements, such as decorative painting on the main-floor ceilings and pastel colors appropriate to the era in which it was built. All of the new finishes are sympathetic to the original marble, oak, and walnut used in 1925. On each subject floor, computers allow access to myriad electronic resources, such as the on-line catalogue, the holdings of CLEVNET, the Internet, and various databases. New and historic reading tables alike include power access through pop-up grommets.

Thanks to Cleveland's Committee for Public Art, the library has an extensive art program. One installation features a mosaic globe, 5 feet in diameter, between the children's literature and the foreign literature departments. Two hundred children, working at ten branch libraries, collaborated

1

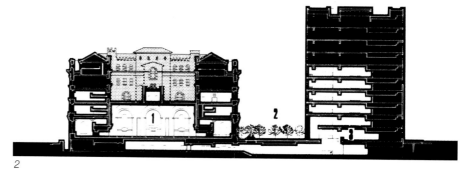

2

1   MAIN BUILDING
2   EASTMAN GARDEN
3   LOUIS STOKES WING

Rockwell Avenue

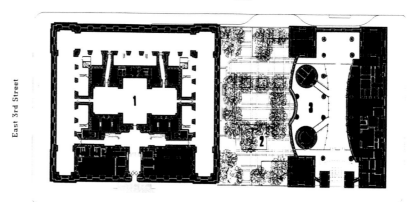

East 3rd Street

East 6th Street

Superior Avenue

20   40   80

3

142

5

7, 8

6

5. Stairwell detail
6. Louis Stokes Wing entry foyer
7. Circulation desk in Stokes Wing
8. Reading room with stenciled ceiling
by artist Holly Morrison
9. Reader tables along periphery of curtainwall
10. Auditorium

9

10

with the artists Anna Arnold, George Bowes, and Lyneise Williams to design the globe's ceramic pieces, whose images reflect the ethnic make-up of their communities.

Louis Stokes Wing

The Louis Stokes Wing, too, follows the 1903 Group Plan and also abides by a later set of city guidelines established for the project in 1992. It is framed by six-story stone pavilions on each corner that match the main library's corner heights and those of the nearby federal courthouse. The marble blocks used for the wing's façade were quarried from the same deposit used for the main library, but the similarity ends there. The pavilions' coursing and patterning, the placement of windows, and its detailing are different from, but respectful of, those of its predecessor. Rising from the stone corners is a ten-story tower equal in height to the adjacent federal reserve bank. The

11

12

11. Bronze gate with sculptural figures designed by Tom Otterness
12. Granite fountain in L-shaped basin by artist Maya Lin and text by Tan Lin
13. Rockwell Avenue façade

wing's convex volume, a departure from the rectangular buildings surrounding it, consists of dramatic floor-to-ceiling frit glass. Each of its four façades differs from the others, a design that allows for a variety of vistas from within the building and for specific features, such as the main entrance, the book drop, a garden view, and servicing to be positioned for maximum ease of use.

The most significant difference between the main library and the Louis Stokes Wing is that the former is inward-looking and the latter faces out toward the city. The main library focuses on Brett Hall, a central interior space that has a courtyard above. Though generous areas of glazing were employed on the building's exterior to illuminate the reading areas along the periphery, its three-story classical columnar façade and high window-sills obstructs the outward view.

The Stokes oval, on the other hand, has focal points on each floor that orient patrons to views beyond the building. The stacks are placed toward the center of each floor, and the reading areas follow the contours of the naturally lit exterior walls. The wing's outward-looking composition pays homage to new technology that extends research capabilities beyond the confines of the library itself. From a distance, the glass oval, a metaphoric lamp of knowledge, identifies the library as a contemporary institution.

The Eastman Reading Garden

In 1937 the city of Cleveland dedicated the area between the main library and the *Plain Dealer* building as the Eastman Reading Garden. A large outdoor reading room, the park had benches, tables with colorful striped umbrellas, and racks of books and magazines for patrons and passersby. Within a few years the park's condition had deteriorated and remained in this state until 1957, when the *Plain Dealer* building became home to the business and science departments of the library, and the library leased the park from the city, launching a campaign to improve it.

The construction of the Louis Stokes Wing and its underground passageway to the main building presented an opportunity for the library to enhance and modestly enlarge the garden. Steel gates with small bronze figures by the sculptor Tom Otterness greet visitors at both of its entrances. A low curving granite wall that echoes the Stokes oval provides seating and serves as a green plinth for the main library. The Olin Partnership, landscape architects, provided an element of choice by encouraging users to move chairs into and out of the series of outdoor rooms defined by plantings. The garden's focus is a quiet fountain and reflecting pool designed by Maya Lin. Paving stones etched with an abstract language poem composed by Tan Lin draw the public into this gentle oasis.

Traditionally, libraries have provided a range of services dedicated to research and reference, unobtrusively expanding to accommodate their patrons' specific information-related needs. Recently, however, libraries have taken on a new role: that of social and cultural center. Along with their routine capabilities, some contemporary libraries now offer places to eat, auditoriums, art galleries, training centers, and public gardens. HHPA's recent work — the expansion and renovation of the Los Angeles Central Public Library (1993), the restoration of Bryant Park behind the New York Public Library (1993), and the renovation of Cleveland's Main Library, new Louis Stokes Wing, and adjacent Eastman Reading Garden — all attest to this new community orientation.

144

THE COLBURN SCHOOL OF PERFORMING ARTS

Los Angeles, California, 1998

The Colburn School of Performing Arts in Los Angeles provides music, dance, and drama education to more than 800 students who range in age from two and a half to eighteen. Once the preparatory division of the University of Southern California's School of Music and housed in a converted warehouse owned by USC, the school today is one of the country's most distinguished performing arts institutions catering to young people.

For more than a decade the school searched for an appropriate site to build a new teaching and performance center. In 1993 it approached the Los Angeles Community Redevelopment Agency about leasing a ⅔-acre parcel on Bunker Hill along Grand Avenue. Its prominent location at the center of downtown's "cultural necklace" adjacent to the Museum of Contemporary Art (MOCA) and the future Disney Concert Hall, near the Los Angeles Music Center, and close to California Plaza's Water Court and Spiral Court, was considered ideal for both students and the city. With its large after-school, evening, and weekend class enrollment, the school greatly contributes to a mixed and vibrant downtown, and prepares its students for professional performance by broadening their exposure to the arts.

HHPA's design for the Colburn School building reflects the variety and excitement of its programs and responds architecturally to its highly visible urban site. The 55,000-square-foot complex sits atop the school's new multistory garage. A landscaped plaza is built over an adjacent side street to connect the Colburn School and MOCA. Not only does the plaza provide an outdoor venue for performance and receptions but it also continues an existing promenade linking California Plaza's other civic offerings.

A main feature of the facility is Zipper Concert Hall, named for Herbert Zipper, a Viennese conductor who organized a secret orchestra in a Nazi concentration camp and, after emigrating to the United States, served as artistic advisor to the Colburn School until his death in 1997. The intimate 420-seat room was acoustically designed for a range of recital and chamber music

1

1. West façade
2. Entry level plan
3. South façade detail
4. South and east façades

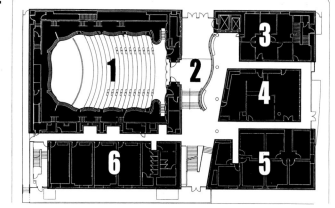

1   CONCERT HALL
2   LOBBY
3   ADMINISTRATION/
    OFFICES
4   RECEPTION/
    LIBRARY
5   STUDIOS
6   CLASSROOMS

10 20   40

2

3

4

5

5. Concert hall seating
6. Herbert Zipper Concert Hall

7

8

programs. Wood trellises incorporating lighting positions and natural terra-cotta materials enhance the room's warmth and elegance.

Another of the school's highlights is the incorporation of the original studio of the violinist Jascha Heifetz, designed by Lloyd Wright in 1946. The hexagonal room was saved from demolition when the artist's house was remodeled and subsequently moved to Colburn's upper level as a special teaching space. The school also features a small recital hall, a variety of teaching studios and practice rooms, classrooms, rehearsal rooms, dance studios, a library, faculty and administrative offices, and lounge areas.

A multilevel lobby and an open stair connect the building's three levels. The lobby space serves as the communal heart and social commons of the school. Students are drawn to the building's center and encouraged to exchange ideas in an informal, light-filled environment. In pleasant weather, they enjoy the multitiered balconies that enliven the building's façade and provide views to the nearby Music Center.

The building's highly geometric profile, height, and siting along the street edge respect the urban character established by the design of its neighbor, MOCA. At the same time, the Colburn School's masonry, metal, and glass cladding assert its own individuality along the streetscape. A modern composition, of Roman bricks and thin horizontal units accented with deeply-raked mortar joints, is juxtaposed with diamond-shaped, zinc-coated shingles that accentuate the concert hall's sloped enclosure. The glass entrance lobby and skylit roof elements further activate the building's presence.

The Colburn School of Performing Arts has become a visual affirmation of the institution's commitment to arts education and the city's urban and cultural agendas. Its vigorous design complements the ambitions of future generations of artists.

7. Dance studio
8. Upper lobby with rebuilt Heifetz studio
9. Lobby at entry level

MARY D. AND F. HOWARD WALSH CENTER FOR PERFORMING ARTS

Texas Christian University
Fort Worth, Texas, 1998

1

The Walsh Center for Performing Arts was carefully designed to achieve three goals: (1) fit in with the neighboring Georgian-style architecture along an arc of the historic turn-of-the-century buildings framing a larger lawn; (2) retain Ed Landreth Hall, an arts center to which it is connected, as the dominant building at the lawn's north end; and (3) have its own identity.

The Walsh Center wraps around Landreth Hall on two sides. A new three-level lobby accessed from two directions and elevations links the two. Complementing the existing auditorium at Landreth, host to prior Van Cliburn International Piano Competition preliminaries, is a new 325-seat recital hall, a 200-seat studio theater, a piano wing, rehearsal rooms, and a music library.

The recital hall is on a diagonal to echo the rotation of the ballet building on the opposite corner of the otherwise symmetrical, original row of campus buildings along the main thoroughfare, University Drive. Its skewed position helps distinguish the Walsh Center within its confined site, and leaves open space for the buildings on either side. Since it faces the formal public lawn, the recital hall closely reflects shapes and materials of other buildings along University Drive. The façade is constructed of limestone, clay block, and travertine in colors similar to adjoining TCU buildings. Because the studio theater faces an interior residential quad, its asymmetrical massing and red granite and red clay block exterior are more prominent, though still in keeping with the campus architecture. These singular volumes are contained within the overall building mass of grooved, yellow brick. Entrances to the complex, through glass and metal porticos, respond to the entry elements found at Landreth Hall.

2

---

1. *Juxtaposition of metal portico and brick*
2. *Scupper detail*
3. *Entry detail*
4. *University Avenue façade with Ed Landreth Hall on right*
5. *Façade facing interior residential quadrangle*
6. *Entry from interior quad*

3

4

5

6

7

154

Working with the acoustical consultant, Jaffe Holden Scarbrough Acoustics, Inc., HHPA devised a new shell-within-a-shell concept for the recital hall. To create an intimate setting for solo and small ensemble performances, the hall is designed as an architectural shell within the larger acoustical volumetric enclosure. This allows sound to filter into the exterior container so that optimal acoustics are achieved in a visually smaller performance area. A dynamic series of diagonal purple and blue profiled wooden ribs, accented with undulating end trim plated with Dutch metal give the interior a theatrical shimmer.

The new asymmetrical thrust stage theater allows varied, three-dimensional arrangements. No seat is more than four rows from the stage. Like the recital hall, a larger volume encloses it, with circulation between building shells. This configuration is useful in training students for film and video performances and for presenting them with challenges in staging, direction, lighting, and design.

With its original use of commonplace campus building materials, new materials, responsive orientation of building masses, and highly distinctive exterior profiles, the new Walsh Center visually ties together generations of TCU architecture in a contemporary form.

7. Entry foyer
8. Ground level plan
9. Lower level plan
10. Hays Studio Theater

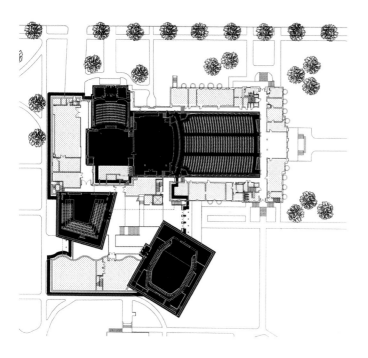

8

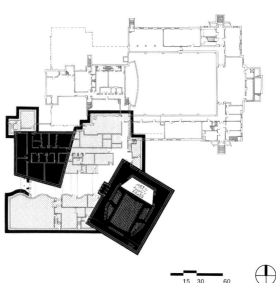

15 30 60

9

11

12

11. Pepsico Recital Hall viewed from circulation
space
12. Recital hall balcony
13. Recital hall

156

U.S. CUSTOMS AND IMMIGRATION CENTER AT RAINBOW BRIDGE

Niagara Falls, New York, 1998

The Niagara Reservation, which encompasses the Falls and adjacent parkland, has the rare distinction of being both a National Historic Landmark and National Natural Landmark. Its incomparable beauty makes it a major tourist destination. In addition to being a scenic attraction, it is home to Rainbow Bridge, the most heavily used point of entry on the northern border of the United States.

In 1990 HHPA won a design competition sponsored by the Niagara Falls Bridge Commission to reconstruct and expand the U.S. Toll Plaza at Rainbow Bridge. The commission desired that the building, through its architecture, be a gift to the community; one that has witnessed the horrors of development in the panorama of the majestic Falls.

Since it was first explored in the eighteenth century, the region has been subjected to an almost unending stream of disfigurements. Though proponents like Frederick Law Olmsted called for the return of the Niagara Gorge to its natural state, influencing its designation in 1885 as the first state park, the process of healing has been slow. Structures, designed to better view the Falls, reach hundreds of feet into the air on the Canadian side and stretch hundreds of feet out into the gorge on the American side, effectually trivializing the natural wonder they were built to observe.

Rainbow Bridge was constructed in l941, on a site just north of the previous Honeymoon Bridge. This refined structure spans 950 feet and consists of two steel arches, each with twenty-four sections. Increased yearly visitation to the Falls challenged the bridge's limited capacity, resulting in long lines of idling vehicles, economic losses for both countries, and a negative air quality assessment. Rather than construct a new bridge, a building program was developed to expand the number of inspection lanes from eight to nineteen and toll lanes from six to eight.

HHPA's original competition-winning design emphasized the economical and efficient processing of incoming vehicular traffic from Canada, while underscoring the grandeur of the site and the dignity befitting its purpose. Facilities for the U.S. Customs Service, the U.S. Immigration and Naturalization Service, and the Niagara Falls Bridge Commission

1

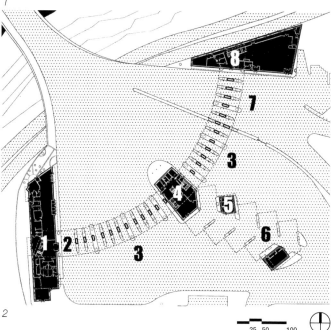

2

25 50   100

3

1. Toll plaza facing the United States
2. Site plan
3. View of toll plaza from under secondary inspection canopy
4. Section through secondary inspection area

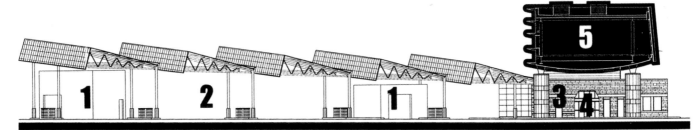

1 INSPECTION GARAGES
2 SECONDARY
   INSPECTION AREA
3 HEAD HOUSE
4 INSPECTION BOOTH
5 MAIN BUILDING

were provided in a 600-foot-long arc of coated dichroic glass (designed with artist Jamie Carpenter), which hovered over the toll plaza. The resplendent, transparent material is responsive to every nuance of light and viewing angle. The intention was to echo the Falls' reflective movement and suggest the transparency and mutability of this natural phenomenon.

160

At the urging of park preservationists, the design was modified to lower the building and eliminate reflective glass, thus reducing its visibility. Nonetheless, it continues to assert itself as a distinctive gateway from one country to the other, and provides a civilized and welcoming approach to Niagara Falls. Design of the Customs and Immigration Building is responsive to both the visual impact when seen from Canada in juxtaposition to the bridge, as well as from the United States.

The concave Canadian façade reflects the graceful structural composition of the bridge and its dramatic setting. By contrast, the convex American façade is shaped and articulated to relate to the more informally arranged adjacent parkland. To provide contextual compatibility, both façades have a series of horizontal and vertical trellises that create plays of light and shadow against the building, similar to those formed in the vegetation of surrounding landscape and by the repetition of bridge supports.

Facing Canada, thin, vertical louvers of perforated metal against frit glass pay homage to the sweeping steel arches of the bridge, and prevent direct sunlight from entering the building. They also allow for unobstructed views of the toll plaza below. Curving away from the viewer, the American façade uses horizontal trellises in pale green, cantilevered from a darker, green glass surface, to harmonize with park views. The layering of trellis members filters sunlight throughout the day. The architectural treatment on both façades increases the visual depth of the enclosure, causing the building mass to recede in effect.

Beneath the span of the 600-foot-long arc are three base buildings built of the same Hamilton bluestone that forms the ledge of the Falls. Openings in their façades are set back to create deep shadows patterned after the scale and texture of the natural rock for-mations lining the river. The materials, height, and massing of the plaza and over-head structures complement the bucolic surround-ings of this significant entry portal. While the U.S. Customs and Immigration Center must be proximate to the Falls and parkland, its simplicity and formality seek to interject a measure of composure to the jumble of man-made intrusions upon the historic landscape.

5. Façade facing Canada

162

6

7

6. Detail of vertical louvers
7. Horizontal trellises atop
bluestone base building
8. View of the building as seen from Canada

SEVEN PROJECTS AT STANFORD UNIVERSITY

Palo Alto, California
1990–1999

164 The historic core of the Stanford University campus is among the most recognizable and memorable academic architecture in the nation. Planned by Frederick Law Olmsted in the late 1880s as a series of formal quadrangles formed by arcaded buildings, the Romanesque style of the original buildings was developed by the architect Charles Coolidge of Boston. Coolidge had been hired in 1883 by Henry Hobson Richardson, and became the lead designer of the successor firm Shepley, Rutan, and Coolidge upon Richardson's death in 1886.

The first campus buildings were erected on Leland Stanford's farm in the early 1890s, and by 1904 many of the central quad's buildings had been completed. These structures featured rusticated sandstone walls, carved stone columns supporting stone arches along the shaded arcades, and sloped red-tile roofs. As most of the construction used unreinforced stone, the great San Francisco earthquake of 1906 did extensive damage to the newly built campus and led to a nearly full reconstruction of the Memorial Church and considerable repairs to many of the other original campus buildings.

In 1989 natural disaster struck again with the Loma Prieta earthquake, which damaged 242 buildings and closed 20. Many of the university's students, faculty, and administrators needed temporary quarters, and the campus recognized that a comprehensive plan for structural strengthening of its historic resources was required both to repair the current damage and to protect the campus from future seismic activity. HHPA has been involved with the campus since 1990 in assisting with the development of guidelines for this effort as well as carrying out the architectural restoration work on a wide range of campus buildings.

1. *Aerial view of historic main quad*
2. *Memorial Church, north façade*
3. *Detail of restored Memorial Church*
4. *Apse of Memorial Church*

1

2

3

5

6

Main Quad Guidelines

Many of the campus' original quad buildings had been adapted over the years, given new mezzanines and layouts that were largely unsympathetic to their historic interiors. Structural strengthening of the historic interiors and exterior arcades also took a variety of approaches up to 1989. HHPA was retained by the university architect, David Neuman, to assist in the development of a consistent set of design guidelines that would define goals and physical recommendations, address life-safety and access needs, and reinforce ways to work with state and federal authorities to gain approval of the reconstruction.

Memorial Church

At the center of the quad is the church Jane Stanford created in memory of her husband, who died in 1893. She worked tirelessly on every aspect of its original design, handpicking Italian tiles and supervising construction, which was completed in 1903. In the 1906 earthquake, just a year after Jane Stanford's death, the church's steeple fell into the sanctuary, blowing out all four walls with its force. The church was rebuilt with steel framing and concrete walls for a 1913 rededication. The one part of the building that was not rebuilt was the remainder of the steeple's base, and the center crossing supporting it below. In 1989 the earthquake caused the crossing to shake loose the mosaic angels at the pendentives and stones in the crossing arches. HHPA's major effort to invisibly strengthen the center portion of the church led to a wealth of behind-the-scenes steel and concrete reinforcement, and the opportunity for a building-wide renovation. Conservation expertise restored the wide range of interior finishes, and new sound and lighting systems were installed to serve the multiuse programs of the church.

Three Quad Buildings

HHPA's first quad renovation was one of its largest buildings, Language Corner (now Pigott Hall), at the southeast corner. Originally it served as the Engineering Building (where Herbert Hoover earned his Stanford degree). Fully restored and modernized, the 44,000-square-foot structure now serves current educational needs. New technologically enhanced classrooms, a multimedia lecture room, faculty offices, and library are contained within the existing shell.

Later HHPA restored the President's and Provost's Building, creating an impressive two story lobby while providing new means of access and installing new systems throughout, and the Center for Race and Ethnicity, a multidisciplinary home for several research centers, including offices, meeting rooms, and computer classrooms.

In 1996 HHPA won a California Preservation Foundation Award for its contributions to preservation technology on these projects.

Cooksey House
On San Juan Hill, near the President's House, is a 1900 shingle style residence which was significantly damaged in the 1989 earthquake. A number of features were rebuilt, such as the impressive entry stair and masonry fireplaces, and the facility was replanned to accommodate a coed cooperative dormitory and to meet current access and technology needs.

Institute for International Studies
Encina Hall was built in 1891 as one of the campus' first buildings, a multiwing building to house the men's dormitory and dining hall. Closed since a 1972 fire, HHPA has rehabilitated its east wing, Encina East, to house research centers, a library, and lounge area for the Institute for International Studies (IIS) — a major multidisciplinary research center for the study of global issues. At Encina Central and Encina South, renovated spaces included additional research areas, a renovated main lobby, and a new conference center for IIS, including teleconferencing rooms and a 300-seat auditorium.

Throughout all of these projects, HHPA has incorporated new structural techniques while recognizing that these projects' success is also determined by attention to interior detail and interpretive design. After having presided for five years over a university with a number of buildings out of service, its president, Gerhard Casper, was pleased to announce at the Pigott Hall dedication, in 1997, "the Quad is back," and Stanford's legacy continues.

5. Encina Hall, east façade
6. Encina Hall, Bechtel Conference Center
7. Pigott Hall stair detail
8. Site plan of quad projects

167

7

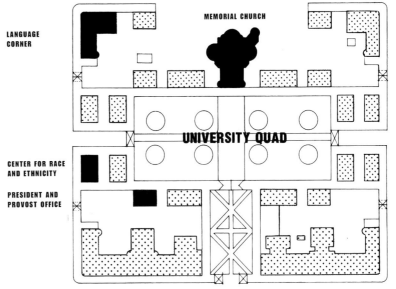

8

LUCILLE "LUPE" MURCHISON PERFORMING ARTS CENTER

**University of North Texas,
Denton, Texas, 1999**

The University of North Texas boasts one of the largest and most highly acclaimed music schools in the country. Students perform in approximately one thousand concerts and recitals yearly. Yet prior to completion of the new Performing Arts Center in 1999, this renowned college of music lacked presence. No campus facility could match the sophistication and the quality of the performances being presented. The dean, David Shrader, had been charged with creating a showcase that would be commensurate with the level of talent it housed. Prior to joining UNT, he had accomplished a similar feat at the University of Nebraska at Omaha, by commissioning HHPA to design the new Weber Fine Arts Building, which opened in 1992.

UNT's 72,500-square-foot building accommodates student concerts, performances by guest artists, musical theater and opera productions, and special events. It houses a 1100-seat concert hall, a 400-seat lyric theater, rehearsal rooms, a music library, a recording studio, scene and costume shops, dressing rooms, green room, administrative offices, a conference room, and storage.

The center's location, on the western edge of the campus along Interstate 35, is highly visible to and easily reached by the several million residents within an hour's drive. As a result, the building becomes a gateway to the university, formally welcoming visitors. Its unique forms and faceted dome make it a recognizable destination as cars approach at high speeds.

Oriented toward Denton's rolling hills and colorful sunsets, the lobby features an immense curved enclosure of glass and illuminated tile walls. Rising out of this space are the concert hall to the north and the lyric theater to the east, both partially clad in Texas limestone. The hall's zinc-tiled roof is distinctive along the skyline and aligns with the main campus cross street on the site. Instrument and choral rehearsal rooms are arranged behind the theater and along the

1.Winspear Concert Hall

2

3

4

concert hall. These and other support spaces are clad in the campus' predominant buff brick with limestone features.

The concert hall is used principally by 20- to 80-member ensembles but can accommodate a 110-piece orchestra and a 150-member chorus. A dozen green-stained wood arches support the hall's red-stained roof decking. Seven chandeliers provide acoustical reflection in addition to illumination. Natural light enters the room from a triple glazed rear stage wall forming both the faceted dome exterior and acoustical interior enclosure.

Traditional and nontraditional opera, drama, and dance performances can be staged in the lyric theater. Both the orchestra pit and main floor seating can be arranged in numerous formats, allowing for proscenium, thrust, or performance-in-the-round. Two surrounding balconies can be used as seating, performance, or technical positions.

The Performing Arts Center is a landmark for Denton and the university, capturing attention along the Interstate, which runs from Laredo to Minneapolis. In addition to cultivating its students' artistic abilities, the facility provides a rich experience for all who attend performances, with exceptional acoustics, public spaces, and striking architectural elements.

2. Lyric theater
3. Lobby
4. Lobby corridor
5. Orchestra level plan
6. Winspear Concert Hall exterior
7. View from Highway I35

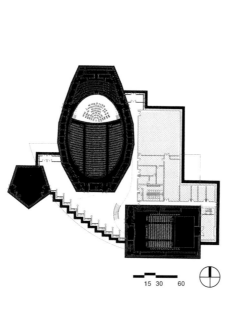

15 30 60

5

6

7

WORKS IN PROGRESS

RADIO CITY MUSIC HALL

New York, New York, 1999

174 Radio City is one of the nation's most famous venues housing some of New York's most awe-inspiring spaces. No other performance hall provides such a combination of history, grandeur, and vast capacity. When it opened, in December, l932, the 5900-seat theater was widely considered to be among the most modern and beautiful in the world. No one had ever seen anything like it: an astonishing design of luxury and sophistication, all for the general public. Its mastermind was Samuel L. ("Roxy") Rothafel, its patron John D. Rockefeller, an incomparable fusion of talents and motivation. Rockefeller was building a monument to the myth of the American capitalistic system in its most trying time—the Great Depression. Roxy was an impresario who understood the public's wish for entertainment in luxurious surroundings, and convinced Rockefeller to build a large hall to present an artistic form of vaudeville, even as this peculiarly American form of entertainment was dying out.

Like Rockefeller Center itself, Radio City's architectural design was the product of collaboration. Three architectural firms, together with many artists and designers, contributed to the dramatic interiors, but it was Donald Deskey's design sense that held everything together in a celebration of American modernism. Now, at the age of sixty-five, the hall is tired, fabrics have faded, and well-meaning attempts at restoration have strayed from the original patterns and colors. Built to celebrate what is new, Radio City has become a pale copy of its original splendor. To satisfy the expectations of twenty-first-century patrons not only must the original finishes be restored, but the original lighting sequences, colors, and intensities must also be enhanced to create the excitement it once inspired.

To reestablish this national landmark as one of the world's premier entertainment facilities, the glamour of the hall's public spaces will be reinstated with the original bold patterns and finishes, original carpet designs, wall coverings, and fabrics. Each mural will be restored to its full brilliance, and original Deskey furniture and fixtures will be put back in place. Most of the original technical systems remain in use, but they will be supplemented by new production

lighting, sound systems, and rigging. A new house curtain matching the original in color and texture will be installed with fiber-optic lighting, permitting a new realm of special effects.

To capture public attention, many of the original design elements of the exterior will be brought back to life to heighten the building's nighttime drama. New marquee lighting with sequenced illumination and the original colors will again identify this as an extraordinary place.

Built to define "what's new," Radio City will again become a contemporary wonder, a home to popular entertainment of great distinction and sophistication. Imbued with Roxy's progressive spirit, this technologically advanced, elegant public hall will welcome a new area of entertainment in high style.

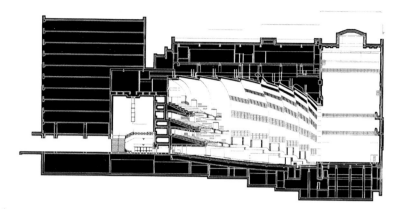

1

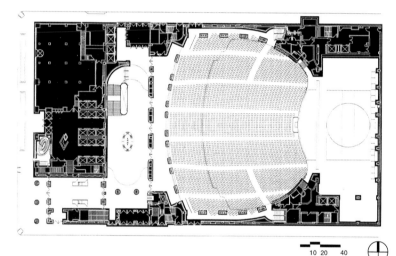

2

10 20 40

1. Section through auditorium
2. Orchestra level plan
3. Marquee, 1945
4. Grand Foyer circa 1932
5. Grand Lounge circa 1934
6. Auditorium circa 1932

3

175

4

5

6

BRIDGEMARKET

New York, New York, 1999

Bridgemarket is an innovative commercial development placed under the Rafael Guastavino vaults of the Queensboro Bridge in Manhattan. This majestic space and historic landmark is being returned, after more than half a century, to its original use as a marketplace. In 1909, when the architect Henry Hornbostle and the engineer Gustav Lindenthal constructed it, the underbelly of the bridge was made into a vibrant, open green market. Rather than leave the roadway structure exposed, its steel cage was camouflaged in a granite and terra-cotta veneer. Interior steel columns were also sheathed in cream-colored terra-cotta rising up to support a canopy of thirty-four tile vaults.

This market under the Queensboro Bridge is widely considered to be one of New York's most dramatic public spaces. Since 1977 HHPA has been working with Bridgemarket Associates to reclaim the structure for public use. Over the past twenty years, the project has slowly evolved, subject to shifting market demands and a complex community review process. Each of the four schemes developed and approved by the Landmarks Commission preserved the integrity of the space while maintaining its ability to adapt to other uses.

Initially the project entailed preservation of Bridgemarket in conjunction with reinstitution of a farmer's market. Inside, retailers would sell prepared foods and products from ground-level stalls, and restaurants would be accommodated on a new mezzanine level. An open-air plaza would contain sheds for a market, a greenhouse, planting area, and a historic fountain. In the mid-1980s the project expanded to include a lower-level retail space, a new freestanding restaurant building, and a farmer's market building. Later, the restaurant building was deleted from the program and the market building relocated on the plaza.

A decade later, Bridgemarket moved into its current phase, which houses three commercial tenants — a Conran's restaurant, a Conran's retail shop, and a Food Emporium market. Together these retailers occupy more than 90,000 square feet of space beneath the bridge. A new 3700-square-foot glass-and-steel, sloped roof pavilion

1

provides a modest showroom along with a dedicated entrance to the lower-level shop. Nighttime illumination allows this transparent, contemporary structure to glow like a display case. Its modernist, refined style captures the spirit of the merchandise designed and selected by Terrance Conran.

A steel-and-glass partition wall that separates the restaurant from the food market divides the ground-floor interior of the vault. Plentiful use of glass enables patrons to see and be seen and enjoy the spectacle of food preparation, enhances visibility of the physical structure, and recalls the open character of the original interior. New curtainwall finish color and framing elements closely match those of the historic exterior.

In Bridgemarket's present configuration, the public is able to fully appreciate the splendor of architectural components as well as the monumental bridge as a whole. Outdoors, on the 59th Street side, there is a landscaped public plaza whose focus is the historic Municipal Art Society fountain, originally located on the southeast bridge pier. The 59th Street entrance is through this plaza, continuing the greenway established along the street to the East River. The lower level, 60th Street entrance accommodates a vehicular drop-off.

2

When complete, Bridgemarket will be a significant urban amenity, unlike any other in New York. Its restoration will create a grand market shop and fashionable dining environment. A catalyst for renewal of the neighborhood, this reclaimed public space will reestablish one of the city's great architectural achievements.

1. Queensboro Bridge circa 1909
2. Structure of entrance pavilion
3. Market under bridge's vaulted arches
4. South elevation

3

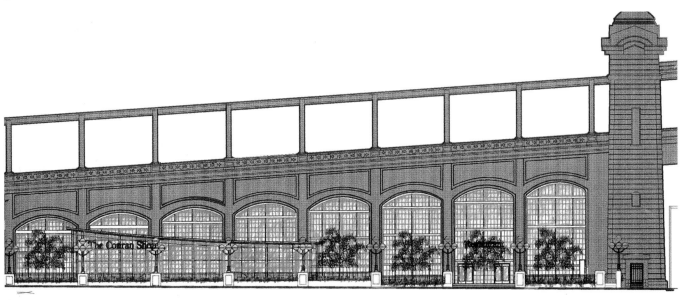

4

15   30   60

SAN ANGELO MUSEUM OF FINE ARTS AND EDUCATION CENTER

San Angelo, Texas, 1999

178 The San Angelo Museum of Fine Arts (SAMFA) was founded in 1981, and formally opened to the public four years later in a restored building at Fort Concho. Not a decade had passed before the museum gained prominence on the national art scene and became host of the Annual National Ceramic Competition, the premier event of its kind in America. Having outgrown its facilities, HHPA was commissioned to design a new museum at the heart of a burgeoning historic, cultural, and economic redevelopment zone.

SAMFA programs extend beyond conventional museum boundaries. The institution serves as a center of culture, education, and entertainment, providing its community with broad access to art exhibitions and educational opportunities. Joining its efforts is Angelo State University, whose art department will conduct regular studio art classes at the museum.

The building's design comprises distinct architectural elements, each oriented to take advantage of its pivotal location. Its long, rectangular plan runs parallel to the city's new Paseo de Santa Angela, a landscaped walkway that connects Fort Concho, a preserved Texas frontier military fort, to the historic downtown across the North Concho River. SAMFA connects directly to River Walk, a several-mile area of continuous pathways and parkland, and it is adjacent to River Stage, an outdoor performance venue. The building's east façade is scaled to respond to the vehicular views from a large thoroughfare, the west elevation engages the character of the developing paseo, while the north end is shaped to look out to the river and the downtown area beyond.

In its elongated shape, materials, color, and texture, the new museum resembles the limestone buildings at Fort Concho. West Texas limestone, quarried nearby, sheathes the mass of the building. Rough-back limestone with weathered and deep pock-marks is used on portions of the building to create shadows and give definition and depth. Blocks of varying color saturation and texture are positioned in striped arrangements. A spavined, copper-clad roof distinguishes the building

1

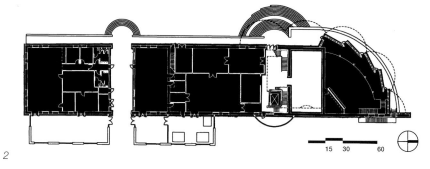

2

from a distance, allowing it to become another of the city's landmarks. Generous, scalloped-shape balconies and a rooftop sculpture garden provide respite and views of the downtown skyline.

The main and upper levels of the museum house flexible galleries of varying sizes. One also functions as an open collections-storage area; another includes a promenade and observation platform. The education center occupies the south wing of the ground floor and can be used by ASU faculty and students twenty-four hours a day without compromising museum security. An outdoor education garden and firing kiln take advantage of San Angelo's climate.

An important component of the program is the museum's 300-seat meeting room,

which doubles as a performance space and which can also accommodate 180 people banquet-style. Superb river views beyond its curved window wall make it ideal for a variety of events, including SAMFA's lecture, chamber music, and film club series. An adjacent caterer's kitchen is equipped with an electric dumbwaiter capable of delivering refreshments to the rooftop garden. Supporting these activities are a gift shop, library, and multilevel lobby.

SAMFA is designed to expand gracefully with the growth of its collections and programs. Acknowledging its civic importance, the building embodies a strong sense of place and pays homage to San Angelo's and west Texas's venerable history.

3

4

5

6

BERRIE CENTER FOR PERFORMING AND VISUAL ARTS

Ramapo College
Ramapo, New Jersey, 1999

1. North façade under construction
2. Site plan
3. Upper level plan
4. South façade under construction
5. Upper level lobby
6. Theater

180 Intended for use by both the college and neighboring communities, the Berrie Center for Performing and Visual Arts, part of the School of Contemporary Arts, will become the most public building on campus. Its prominent site is the fourth side of an implicit quadrangle that is defined on two sides by metal-and-glass structures and on the third by an 1890 mansion converted for administration.

The 54,000-square-foot center comprises four geometric volumes, each distinguished by its own roofline and materials. These distinct elements relate to surrounding academic buildings and established green space. A long, low rectangular volume faces the quadrangle; its metal and glass façade responds to adjacent campus buildings. This wing houses galleries, classrooms, practice rooms, studios, and shops as well as administration and faculty offices.

The other three building forms — a 350-seat proscenium theater, a rehearsal/performance space, and a 100-seat studio theater — intersect the rectangle. Like the mansion, these public areas are clad in masonry. Their unique volumetric shapes identify them from the exterior as significant program spaces for experimental art. Where they intersect the metal and glass enclosure, their walls and cladding materials continue on the interior, giving definition to the multistoried lobby that links all activities.

Because of its sloping site, entrances are provided on two levels. The upper level entrance is framed by the studio theater and rehearsal space, the lower level is circumscribed by the enclosure of the proscenium theater. A circle intersecting the ground floor plan gives shape to outer lobby walls. It continues beyond the confines of the structure to define a plaza along the building's edge.

The Berrie Center will offer state-of-the-art facilities for video art, electronic music, computer art, digital imaging, virtual reality, and a range of multimedia applications. Its design embodies one of the school's major objectives: to give students an understanding of the way art tools can be used for communication and expression.

1

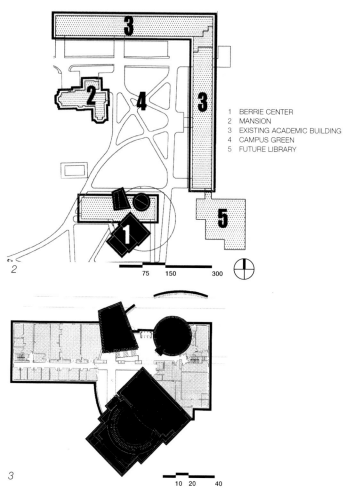

2

1 BERRIE CENTER
2 MANSION
3 EXISTING ACADEMIC BUILDING
4 CAMPUS GREEN
5 FUTURE LIBRARY

75   150   300

3

10 20   40

4

5

6

RITTER HALL

**University of California, San Diego
Scripps Institution
of Oceanography
San Diego, California, 1999**

182 Scripps Institution of Oceanography (SIO) is one of the oldest, largest, and most important centers for global science research and graduate school coursework in the world. Now part of the University of California, San Diego, it has maintained its own campus on 770 acres of coastal property since the turn of the century. Ritter Hall, which houses several of the Institution's scientific programs, is among its earlier buildings. To better support the sophisticated research activities that occur there, HHPA and Ehrlich-Rominger were commissioned to renovate the historic structure and design a freestanding building as part of the Ritter laboratory complex. When it is complete, it will be one of SIO's primary scientific laboratory and teaching facilities, as well as home to its distinguished and extensive Marine Vertebrate Collection.

The original Ritter Hall, designed by the southern California architects Irving and Louis Gill in 1931, is an example of the simplified Mission style architecture Irving Gill pioneered in the La Jolla area. It is a companion to his Scripps Memorial Laboratory, also modern in treatment, which, when it opened 1912, was SIO's and La Jolla Shores's first structure.

Over the years several unsympathetic additions made to the SIO campus near Ritter Hall obstructed views of the landmark Scripps laboratory. To preserve the lab's visual prominence, a 1959 L-shaped expansion will be demolished and the replacement set into the hillside on axis with the original. This substitution creates a new park at the heart of the campus, maximizes views of the Pacific, and reinforces the orthogonal grid along which buildings face shoreline piers.

The design of the new 54,000-square-foot building is premised on the importance of the interaction among researchers and specialists. HHPA developed a U-shaped laboratory plan, placing the larger, laboratory component behind a wing of three low-scaled office units and a conference room. These rectangular office blocks are angled relative to the plan of the labs to face the new green space and ocean beyond, and open onto an atrium that links offices and

1

labs, offering a light-filled area for impromptu meetings.

Natural ventilation is a significant element of the design. To take advantage of ocean breezes each office has its own operable windows and the atrium is open on all sides.

The concrete-block building has a rich array of finishes that relate to the nautical environment. Three triangular translucent roofs, which cover the outdoor atrium, are reminiscent of ship sails. Teakwood window frames with matching trellises help filter the strong western sunlight. Stainless-steel stanchions and steel cables support the teak railings that line the stairways and atrium.

The creation of internal and external gathering places where students and researchers can communicate without technology and share ideas in an open and informal environment is an essential element of the design. These spaces complement the state-of-the-art laboratories that support investigations into global climate change and the relationship of the oceans to the earth, the atmosphere, and life. The fully renovated Ritter Hall and the new research, conference, and office building coupled with new parklands, courtyards, and covered outdoor spaces will result in an efficient and comfortable setting for scientific inquiry.

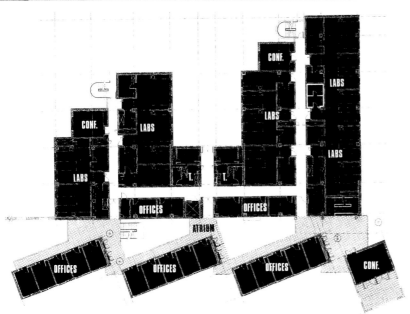

1. Detail of window trellises
2. Elevation facing new green space
3. First floor plan

CONF.

LABS

CONF.

LABS

LABS

LABS

LABS

T.

T.

OFFICES

OFFICES

ATRIUM

OFFICES

OFFICES

OFFICES

CONF.

8   16   32

2

3

WHITAKER CENTER FOR SCIENCE AND THE ARTS

Harrisburg, Pennsylvania, 1999

184 The Whitaker Center for Science and the Arts is intended to be an epicenter for central Pennsylvania's cultural life. Upon completion, the new 130,000-square-foot building will be the first in the nation to combine science and arts activities in a single facility. It will house a mix of scientific, artistic, cultural, and educational presentations, programmed to appeal to a broad cross-section of the city's population.

Major components of the center are a 600-seat proscenium theater, a 39,000-square-foot Science Center, and a 200-seat IMAX film theater. Each of these elements is physically represented in the building's distinctive design. The center's corner location, between Market and Third Streets and Strawberry Square, a heavily traversed downtown area, and near a major hotel and commercial and retail center, required an active exterior to arouse curiosity about the range of attractions it offers.

A dramatic, sloping roofline catches the eye and helps relate the Whitaker Center to varied building heights along Market Street. Illuminated pylons punctuate the building's two public façades, increasing its visibility day and night. Mottled sandstone encases the principal program elements and continues through to the interior. Its warm color, rough fractured facing, and variegated texture give depth to the structure. Rotated within the building's mass is a three-story lobby with a patterned slate exterior in pale gray, green, and red. Its translucent metal dome filters sunlight during the day; at night, it becomes a lantern that animates the streetscape.

Large glass areas also activate the façade, offering interior views and inviting participation. Inside, a two-story public walkway arcs through the building, visually connecting its disparate architectural forms and three primary entrances. The civic "front door" is on Market Street, where pedestrians enter and a vehicular drop-off is provided. The theater entrance is in the lobby and patrons ascend a grand stair for entrance to the museum, IMAX theater, and theater mezzanine. Rehearsal and classroom areas on the lower level can be directly approached from Third Street. Visitors arriving from Strawberry Square and the

1

neighboring garage also have direct entry through Strawberry Arcade, a pedestrian thoroughfare.

The theater accommodates a variety of performance types produced by local arts organizations. Two balconies and orchestra-level seating bring intimacy to both small and full-capacity audiences. The Science Center consists of permanent and traveling exhibition space for interactive learning experiences, flexible classroom/demonstration areas, and a gift shop. The large-format film theater presents three-dimensional IMAX films, which support and complement the center's programs. A sweeping public lobby, a large part of which can be closed off for private engagements, links these features and various entrances.

The Whitaker Center will be a dominant presence within the landscape of the Capital Region. Its distinctive shape, electronic signage, and vigorous illumination will make this structure and all it offers a focal point for the community.

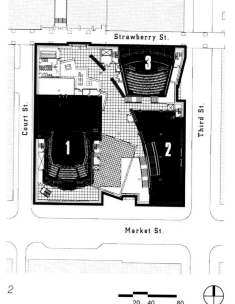

2

20 40 80

1. Model of Market Street façade
2. Site plan
3. Model of Market Street façade at night
4. Market Street entrance under construction
5. Market Street façade under construction

185

3

4

5

EVO A. DeCONCINI FEDERAL BUILDING AND UNITED STATES COURTHOUSE

Tucson, Arizona, 1999

In 1995 HHPA was selected as part of the General Services Administration's Design Excellence program, in association with the firm Leo A. Daly, to design a new federal building and courthouse that would meet the requirements of the U.S. Courts and related federal agencies in the Tucson community for the next thirty years. The DeConcini building will replace the 1953 James A. Walsh Federal Courthouse and consolidate court functions in a secure, safe, and welcoming environment.

HHPA's master plan provides for 413,000 square feet of new courthouse and office space on a 4-acre site at the corner of a major intersection leading to the heart of downtown. The property lies within the city's central business area, adjacent to the civic center and other government office buildings to the north and northeast. The building's design encourages public access across the site in anticipation of further development to the south and southwest.

HHPA developed a design that conveys the stability and dignity of the judiciary system. The varied façades of the building allude to its interior program. Two six-story wings in an L-shape are tied together by a faceted glass- and metal-panel public circulation corridor. Colored plaster sheathes the courtrooms, while their support functions are made of ashlar-patterned concrete block and glass. Complementing the wings are a series of articulated programmatic elements. A translucent exterior canopy supported by overscaled terra-cotta columns penetrates the corner of the building and becomes its monumental entry. Public elevators are contained in a vertical bar attached to the southwest side of the building, and a cylinder houses jury assembly space.

The building features loggias, overhangs, alcoves, and deeply set windows that mitigate Tucson's extreme environmental conditions. Areas of the building that are occupied throughout the day face north and east; those with transitional occupancy, such as the circulation corridors, are oriented to the south and west to limit exposure to intensive sunlight. Corrugated metal panels along public corridors serve as sunshade devices without obstructing views of the

1

courtyard below and Sentinel Mountain beyond. The wing on the north of the building offers pedestrians a generous arcade.

The wings are organized around two interconnected courtyards. The heavily landscaped area on southwest side of the building is referred to as the Winter Courtyard, as it will receive the afternoon sunlight and be a popular gathering place during that mild and temperate season. In the heat of the summer, the building will shade the landscaped area on the northeast side for most of the day. Each courtyard has different program objectives; one marks the procession from informal to formal space with use of ceremonial stairs, and the other provides an opportunity for public gathering and weekend recreational use.

The building is being designed to allow for the future conversion of offices into courtrooms and chambers to accommodate an increasing judicial workload—HHPA's master plan, based on expected 2022 space requirements, includes a future 150,000-square-foot office building to house federal tenants.

For the current building, the program includes fourteen courtrooms, judicial chambers, a library, conference rooms, the judges' dining facility, a media/press room, jury assembly areas, a childcare center, and a public cafeteria. It also provides office suites and support space for federal tenants.

The new Federal Building and U.S. Courthouse is responsive to its desert setting, and its interior design incorporates the textures, colors, and materials found in Tucson's natural landscape. The building's horizontal massing and surface treatment also reflects the southwestern vernacular. When it opens to the public, in 1999, the building will complement the downtown civic area, in which it will sit, encourage public use, and stand as testament to the permanence and accessibility of our judicial system.

In 1996 the General Services Administration conferred upon HHPA a Design Award for Building in Progress. At the time the project was also noted for having the lowest cost per square foot of any new courthouse built under the auspices of the GSA's Design Excellence Program.

---

1. Main entrance
2. Southwest façade with Winter Courtyard under construction
3. Detail of east façade
4. Street level plan

2

3

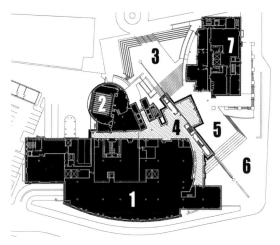

4

1 DISTRICT WING
2 JURY ASSEMBLY
3 WINTER
   COURTYARD
4 LOBBY
5 OUTDOOR
   CEREMONIAL
   LOBBY
5 SUMMER
   COURTYARD
7 BANKRUPTCY
   WING

30 60   120

FITERMAN HALL

**Borough of Manhattan
Community College
New York, New York, 2000**

In 1993 Shirley and Miles Fiterman, two patrons of the arts, donated a 1959 fifteen-story office building, designed by William Lescaze, to Manhattan Community College, part of the City University system. The site is adjacent to a number of New York City's greatest resources: the World Trade Center, the artistic communities of Tribeca and SoHo, Wall Street, and City Hall. Among these attractions, the academic building must assert its own identity as a place for higher learning and career development.

The newly acquired 360,000 square feet of space presented an opportunity to alleviate the college's severe shortage of computer labs and state-of-the-art classrooms. Conversion of a standard, corporate office building into an inviting and heavily used academic building posed several challenges.

Unlike office workers who enter during rush hour in the morning, students enter Fiterman Hall in surges throughout the day. More than 8000 people access the building daily (twice as many as the population for which it was designed), and during peak activity 2600 enter within a fifteen-minute period. HHPA developed new vertical and horizontal circulation plans to accommodate the demand for egress.

Fiterman Hall includes a new corner entrance, visible from the college's main building a few blocks east, a two-story volume that leads to a range of amenities. From two sides, students enter and can directly go to a three-story Technology Resource Center, student lounge, dining commons, art gallery, and central information bank. One level down there is a student union, and the "family college" for children of BMCC students is on the second floor. These easily reached facilities disperse the overflow of people entering at one time, and invigorate the college's street-level presence. The ground level is also open to the Wall Street community, which enhances the mix of people and the general character of the space.

Eight new high-speed elevators are programmed at peak hours to make limited stops. To reach floors in between, students will use open convenience stairs. Foot traffic relieves congestion and encourages

1

interaction. Floors three through fifteen contain 150 classrooms, quiet study lounges, computer labs, and more than 50 offices and conference rooms. Each classroom and lab permits connections to broadcast, cable, closed-circuit TV, and networked computers.

On the exterior, these floors are defined by alternating bands of black and silver window mullions, set against planes of white brick and black granite perimeter columns, which emphasize the building's layered appearance. This neutral exterior serves as a contemporary foil for the glow of colorful interiors. Articulation of the base includes a new jagged, two-story curtain wall, above which the building's upper mass appears to float. The postminimalist conceptual artist Robert Barry embellished the wall with words chosen by students and faculty, such as "unity," "believe," and "communicate."

One enters through a light-filled, dynamic lobby. While the exterior is reskinned in refined tones, the interior exudes youthful variety and exuberance. Bright blue columns, a ceiling defined by wood ripples stippled with lights, multicolored glass-block panels by artist Arland Huang, and a 150-foot-wall of corrugated, perforated metal animate the interior expanse. Other commissioned artwork, display cases,

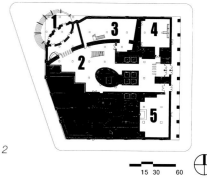

2

15 30 60

kiosks, and video monitors further enliven the space.

The restrained sophistication of the exterior improvements in conjunction with a lively interior palette and contemporary use of materials celebrates the vivacity and purpose of BMCC students. Together with all new building systems and advanced technological capabilities, Fiterman Hall will become a valuable and integral extension of the institution's primary campus.

1. Renovated façade
2. Street level plan
3. Building axonometric

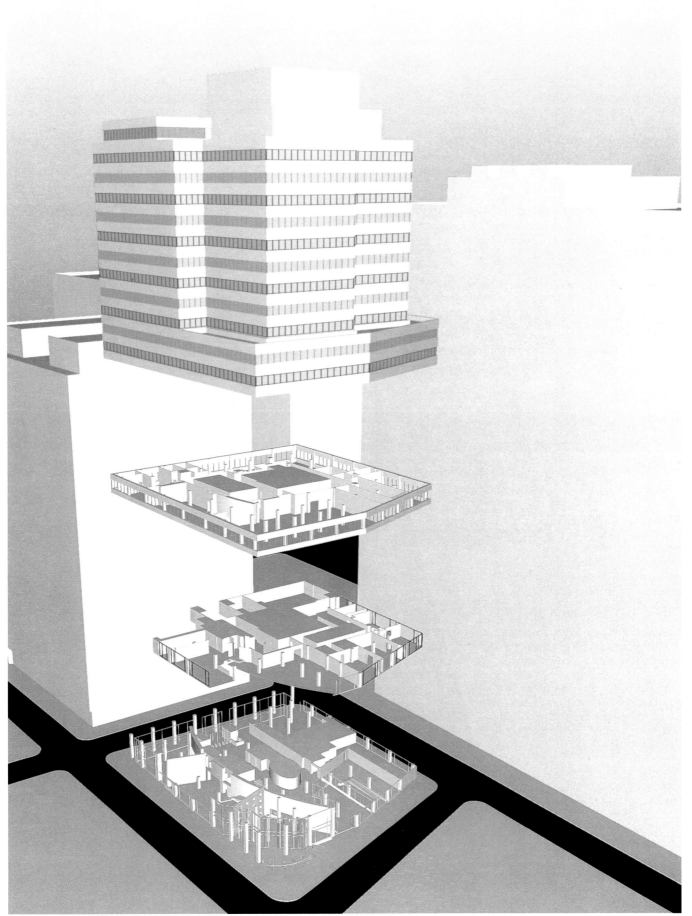

MARTHA RIVERS AND E. BRONSON INGRAM LIBRARY

Vassar College
Poughkeepsie, New York, 2000

190 Vassar College's wooded 1000-acre campus is renowned for the beauty of its grounds and the variety of its architecture. Since its founding in 1861, more than one hundred residential and academic facilities have been built in styles ranging from neo-Gothic to Victorian to classical to modern and to post-modern by such architects as James Renwick, Marcel Breuer, and Eero Saarinen.

The Frederick Ferris Thompson Memorial Library, which HHPA was commissioned to renovate and expand, was designed in 1905 by Allen and Collens in an English perpendicular style. Unlike the architects' discreet, colonial revival gymnasium at Bowdoin College (which HHPA converted into a student union in 1995), the library's imposing stature often causes it to be mistaken for a church by campus visitors.

Since it opened the library has been joined by several additions including Van Ingen Hall (1937), which now houses the art library, and Lockwood Library (1976), which provides space for the college's collection and its rare books and manuscripts. Its original composition includes a massive central tower, three elongated wings, and a grand entrance hall. One of its most noted features is a stained-glass window depicting the first conferral of a doctorate on a woman, Elena Lucrezia Cornaro Piscopia, at the University of Padua, in 1678. Though incremental expansion accommodated growth of holdings and services, clear circulation was sacrificed, and users frequently became disoriented.

HHPA's master plan for the library reorganizes and expands facilities while integrating digital technology with the book and print-based culture. Renovation and expansion adds clarity of organization and space for traditional library services, provides access to new technologies, and offers plentiful programmed areas for the socializing, interaction, and discussion so vital in the electronic age. Improvements include electronic facilities for research and teaching; enhanced reference and reader services; networked computer workstations; special-collections archives; group study/viewing rooms; more than eighty-five faculty studies; additional reading rooms and seating areas; and an exterior

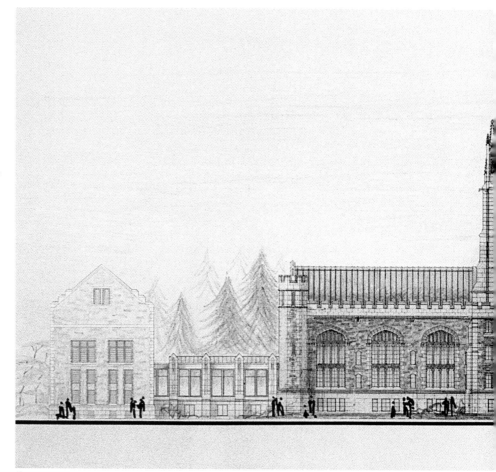

1

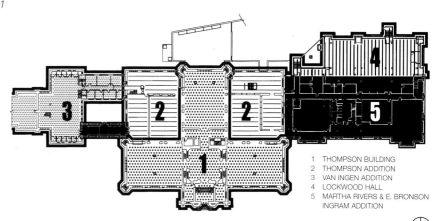

2

1 THOMPSON BUILDING
2 THOMPSON ADDITION
3 VAN INGEN ADDITION
4 LOCKWOOD HALL
5 MARTHA RIVERS & E. BRONSON INGRAM ADDITION

15 30   60

courtyard with network connections and moveable seating.

Design of the addition preserves and honors the integrity of the existing building without repeating it, and helps unify the assemblage of styles in the quad whose west side the library occupies. The vocabulary of materials similar to the original include mottled limestone at the base and a standing-seam copper roof. Red and burgundy bricks arranged in a diamond composition enliven the addition's façade and complement the patterned surface of Rockefeller Hall, a neighboring classroom building. The expansion and new connection between

Van Ingen and Thompson respond to the fenestration, base, spires, and piers of the original in massing, scale, and rhythm to create a cohesive whole. This link enhances the longitudinal plan from Lockwood to the Frances Lehman Loeb Art Center, strengthening its relationship to the monumental main building directly opposite.

With new electronic information technologies, abundant gathering places, increased space for collections, more efficient and better defined circulation, and improvements to building systems, the library will be able to continue its rich tradition of service well into the next century.

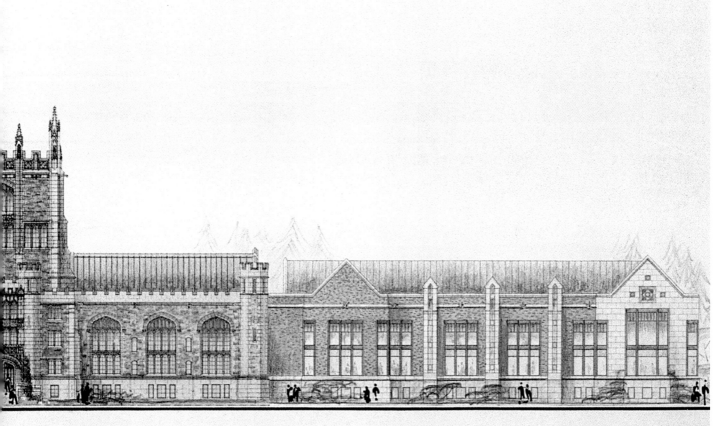

191

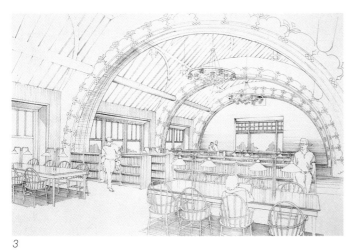

3

4

1. West elevation
2. Ground level plan
3. Periodical reading room
4. Multimedia complex

SOKA UNIVERSITY OF AMERICA

Aliso Viejo, California, 2001

1. Dormitory under construction
2. Dormitory plan
3. View of central campus courtyard facing library

192 The first phase of the new Soka University of America campus is now under construction, implementing the program and master plan concepts developed by HHPA in 1996. This increment comprises nine buildings and is terraced within the scenic, hilltop terrain of Wood Canyon. When the first class is admitted, in 2001, students will interact with an academic environment that feels complete, though in its early stage of development.

Each building is a contemporary interpretation of the Mediterranean style. Smooth stucco exteriors accented with travertine detailing in like color, flat terra-cotta roof shingles, and deep, heavy timber eaves form the primary palette. Monolithic Italian travertine is used for the surrounds at major entrances and the many colonnades that grace the campus. Retaining walls also incorporate stucco and travertine. Decomposed granite is used to surface quiet outdoor areas while porphyry pavers mark pathways and building entries.

Visitors enter the campus core through the library, one of the university's most significant structures. A grand flight of steps leads through the angled building under a monumental arch. Library services are housed in the left wing, with computing and media services to the right. Above the arch, on the fourth floor, is the formal reading room that can double as a venue for special events. Upper level decks offer views of the lily ponds and main plaza at the heart of the campus core. The facility has a variety of seating configurations, a computer writing classroom, a multimedia room, twenty-four-hour study areas, a copy center, and conference rooms.

Across from the library is the University Center. Designed for phased implementation, it is the campus focal point and links student housing and the academic core. The three-story building houses food court–style dining areas in the lower level and opens onto the central plaza for outdoor dining and receptions. At the upper terrace level is a bookstore, a mailroom, and a coffee bar. Other amenities in the center include a conference suite, counseling and medical services, and meeting rooms. Students can "see and be seen" on an open-air stair that connects all levels.

1

2

The President's and Dean's Classroom Buildings are similar in program. Both contain the office of their namesake as well as learning clusters comprised of a classroom, a seminar room, and three faculty offices. This teaching module is the keystone of Soka's highly personal pedagogy. The President's building holds larger classroom spaces while the Dean's Building has science labs, a fine arts wing, and a large presentation/lecture room. Both three-story buildings feature arcades that provide direct access to classrooms. The interior side arcade faces an upper courtyard at plaza level while the arts wing arcade faces a lower courtyard. Each courtyard is wired for technology. A wing proposed for the President's Building will reinforce the orientation of classroom buildings designated in later phases.

Tiered steps designed to encourage interaction among students lead from the University Center to the residence halls. Three types of housing are planned, each interconnected by terraced gardens and courtyards. In phase one, freshmen live in traditional dormitories that include double bedrooms, living rooms, a computer/study room, a multipurpose room equipped with a kitchen, and an exercise room. Future phases will include lodge-style units for sophomores and juniors that are modeled on expanded single-family homes with double and single bedrooms. Seniors and married students will enjoy private apartments. A recreation center near the campus entry will provide exercise and athletic facilities.

Each of these buildings fits aesthetically within the dramatic natural setting. Plazas and green spaces link public and ceremonial buildings with those that are private and informal. Every twist of the landscape brings with it spaces that enhance social development and global understanding, the foundations of Soka's philosophy.

INFORMATION SERVICES BUILDING AND HOCKEN LIBRARY

University of Otago
Dunedin, New Zealand, 2001

194 Founded in 1869, the University of Otago is New Zealand's oldest and the world's southernmost university. The original campus includes a well-preserved group of Gothic and Victorian stone buildings. As the university expanded in the 1960s and 1970s, a second generation of buildings was constructed consisting of numerous stark, concrete-clad high-rises. HHPA is now defining the university's third generation of architecture, which is distinctively modern.

HHPA's design of the new Information Services Building (ISB) reweaves the campus fabric by using an architectural vocabulary and landscape approach that defines a new era. The ISB is a major addition to the central library at the southwest corner of the campus with a new enclosed link to the University Union. When complete in 2001, the old and new structures will be an integrated and harmonious composition of glass. The ISB is also the centerpiece of a new student precinct developed simultaneously in an HHPA master plan. By grouping buildings and landscaped areas into a cohesive plan, HHPA created a student-centered learning environment — a place to interact with electronic information, the university, and each other.

A key element of the design is the linking of library services to the existing University Union to house a new twenty-four-hour "information marketplace." At the heart of this part of the ISB are amenities such as training, seminar, and group-study areas; lounge seating; print-and-copy centers; Internet terminals; wired carrels; and computer stations. The ground level accommodates the majority of library staff to easily provide assistance, and connects to the union via a two-story link. This major circulation route through campus contains three kiosks with concessions at ground level and conference suites above. A new campus store, lockers, touch-screen information systems, and café seating are also provided.

There are two entry points to the secure areas of the ISB, allowing access to the two upper levels which house book collections, reading areas, staff areas, and group-study areas.

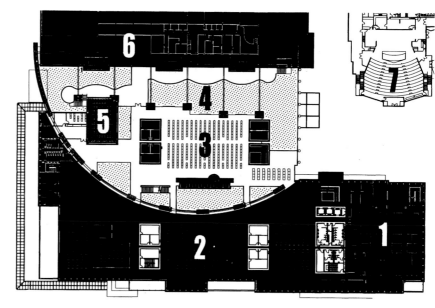

1

1 COLLECTION MANAGEMENT
2 COLLECTIONS
3 PERIODICALS
4 THE LINK
5 RARE BOOK
6 EXISTING STUDENT UNION
7 EXISTING LECTURE HALL

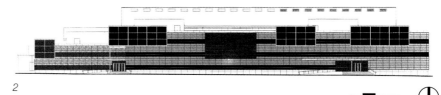

2

15 30 60

The building's façade is composed of bands of frosted and clear glass topped by two-story interior glass boxes. Passersby can watch the bustle of activity within the ISB through its transparent skin. In late afternoon and evening the well-lit building becomes a beacon.

In addition to glass, HHPA's design incorporates Oamaru stone that is quarried locally and used on many of the campus' historic buildings. At the ISB, large split blocks are used to give texture to the interiors. Two 70-foot pylons, which support a twenty-first-century timepiece at the entrance to the building, the colonnade extending from the union to the ISB, and a major interior curved wall that defines an edge of the light-filled atrium are all constructed of this stone. To further enhance the connection to historical architecture on campus, a blue stone found in several university buildings is also used. Customarily

the stone is used in its rough state. However, here the architects are smoothing it and laying it as paving for the link and plaza adjacent to the ISB.

Working with Opus International on all the Otago projects, HHPA has also renovated the University's Science Library and converted a 1930s Art Moderne cooperative dairy into the new Hocken Library, a repository for New Zealand's finest historic photos, manuscripts, artwork, and books. The facility includes a lobby for receptions, a café, reading room, art gallery, workshops, and information commons. This project, completed in 1998, is the result of a master plan that HHPA developed for the campus-wide upgrade of libraries to achieve an information technology-rich environment throughout the university.

1. Second level plan
2. South elevation
3. New ISB addition and link
to University Union
4. Model detail of ISB south façade
5. ISB atrium with information commons

195

3

4

5

ATLANTIC CENTER

Brooklyn, New York, 2002

196   Atlantic Center is a 750,000-square-foot retail development atop Brooklyn's busiest rail transportation hub, Atlantic Terminal. For thirty years following a 1956 attempt to develop the property as the new Ebbetts Field and home of the Dodgers, the site remained vacant. Though designated an urban renewal area by the city in 1968, the lot was not developed until 1995 when phase one of Atlantic Center opened. HHPA's design of phase two adds retail and entertainment facilities to this bustling complex.

Atlantic Center is a key component in the ongoing renovation of downtown Brooklyn. Its site, at the edge of the development district, is pivotal. First, it is situated at the confluence of three of Brooklyn's main traffic arteries; second, it is just south of the Brooklyn Academy of Music historic district; and third, and most significantly, it is located directly above Atlantic Terminal, which serves 50 million subway and railroad commuters yearly. Before this phase of the center's evolution, this enormous number of retail shoppers had limited amenities and conveniences.

Phase two of Atlantic Center encompasses a major department store, retail shops, a twelve-screen cineplex, and an outdoor piazza with public seating and commercial kiosks. Each façade of the three-story building responds to the character of its immediate streetscape. Portions of the building facing residential neighborhoods are more modest in scale, while the prominent curved façade along Flatbush Avenue emphatically embraces the streetwall. To tie together varying site influences, a rich and distinctive palette of materials was developed. The predominantly masonry mass defers to neighboring brownstones. Precast concrete details relate to the buff-colored limestone of the bank, directly opposite. A green metal cornice delineates the building's upper story, which is sheathed in a combination of corrugated and flat metal panels.

Rising next to Brooklyn's tallest building and most heavily used transportation hub, Atlantic Center will soon become downtown's largest retail facility. HHPA's spirited design celebrates the flourishing of this centerpiece site, which has so long been ready for development.

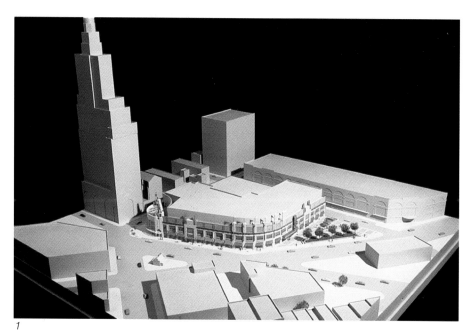

1

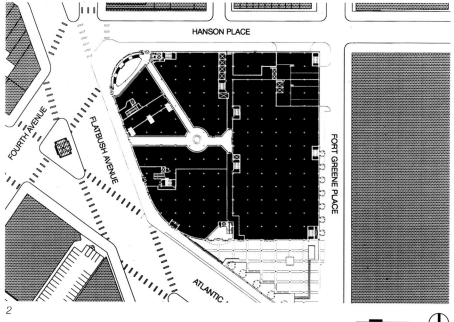

2

25   50   100

3

PLANNING PROJECTS

METROPOLITAN STATION MASTER PLAN

Los Angeles, California, 1993

The long-range plan developed by HHPA for Metropolitan Station proposed to transform 47 acres of abandoned Southern Pacific railway yards into a campus for public- and private-sector offices, retail facilities, a theater, a restaurant, a hotel, housing, entertainment, and recreation. Located just north of downtown Los Angeles, adjacent to Chinatown, Elysian Park, and Dodger Stadium, the site is easily accessible by car and mass transit. The challenge in redeveloping the property was to integrate it with the residential neighborhood to its north and provide a buffer between it and an industrial area to the south.

The goal was to create an open space landscape environment while insuring an economically viable level of development. Several distinctive facilities on the southern perimeter of the site will contain nearly 3 million square feet of commercial office space designed to suit the needs of major headquarter tenants. A significant retail component is also proposed, along with more than 700 units of residential housing along the northern edge of the property. Parking for 7000 vehicles is discreetly tucked under the slope of the site, just below the retail and residential zone.

A key feature of the plan is a central spine of public and private courtyards, open spaces that link each neighborhood. Metropolitan Court, a large tree-lined plaza, defines the entry to Metropolitan Station. Public green spaces continue to Metropolitan Steps, a proposed bustling open-air center with a variety of amenities, including a light-rail transit station, informal seating, food vendors, and kiosks.

The first phase of development was planned to include a new headquarters for a major public utility, the site's primary tenant. Several interconnected low-rise buildings, totaling 627,000 square feet, are grouped around a secure open courtyard. The executive boardroom and auditorium, employee cafeteria, daycare center, and health/fitness facility encircle the landscaped enclosure. Ground-level arcades alongside buildings provide a human-scale, pedestrian environment.

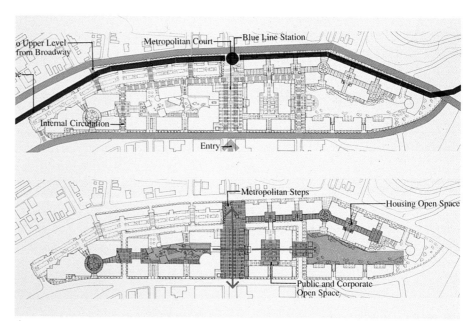

1

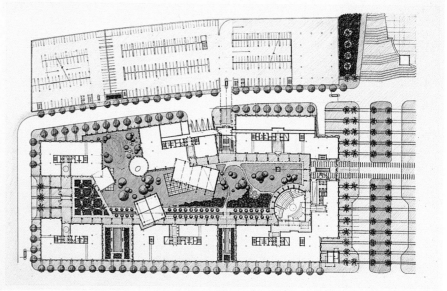

2

Metropolitan Station, as envisioned, incorporated an appropriate balance of employment, housing, and recreational opportunities. In addition to providing a humane environment in which to live and work, the development sought to make a significant contribution to the "Rebuild Los Angeles" program by planting a well-placed seed for the growth of surrounding neighborhoods.

1. Transportation and urban design/open space plans
2. Phase I site plan
3. Proposed headquarters building and campus entry
4. Aerial of proposed development

3

4

WARNER BROS. HOLLYWOOD STUDIOS COMPREHENSIVE DEVELOPMENT PLAN

West Hollywood, California, 1993

202 Since 1980 the Warner Bros. Hollywood Studios have housed Warner Bros. television and film production and postproduction activities. Its rich history, initally as the United Artists Studio and later as the Samuel Goldwyn Studio, however, dates back to 1919 when the first in a line of Hollywood's legendary actors and producers, including Mary Pickford, Douglas Fairbanks, Charlie Chaplin, D. W. Griffith, and Samuel Goldwyn, began filming on the site.

The 10-acre property, on Santa Monica Boulevard between Formosa Avenue and Poinsettia Place, has been designated as eligible for listing in the National Register. HHPA developed a comprehensive development plan that articulates architectural and streetscape improvements to make the studio more prominent in the community and to modernize facilities within the streetwall to support contemporary production needs.

Special attention is given to maintaining the historic character of the Santa Monica Boulevard elevation while enhancing its aesthetic and pedestrian appeal. Two elevator towers linked by an upper-level footbridge become a new gateway announcing entry into the lot. The bridge provides passage between new parking and office facilities. An expansive mural depicting historic and current studio images and ground-floor retail are incorporated into the façade of the parking structure to obscure interior views of vehicles. Exhibition areas in the base of the towers celebrate the history of the studio and early days of Hollywood filmmaking. New towers at both ends of the property provide visitor orientation and retail amenities. Their architectural character is reminiscent of the original tower in the 1920s Santa Monica building.

1

2

Other urban design elements include a studio "walk," with bronze plaques commemorating movies filmed at the lot implanted in the pavement. Openings in the studio streetwall with wrought iron insets allow views into courtyards and landscaped areas behind. Also, part of the city's one percent for art program will create Howard Hughes Court, featuring decorative paving, landscaping, and a replica of the vintage car driven by the multifaceted studio executive.

HHPA's plan provides standards and guidelines for the development of new facilities as well as the preservation of existing historic structures within the lot. The scale and treatment of architectural elements reinforce the traditions and glamour of Hollywood's movie industry. Construction of four new sound stages, 285,000 square feet of office space, and more than 100,000 square feet of postproduction facilities is planned for phased implementation.

Neighborhood workshops were conducted to gain consensus on the development plan. Key to the community's support were plans for the preservation and relocation of the Formosa Café, a local cultural landmark. The expansion program not only satisfies operational requirements and enhances the studio's visual appeal but also ensures future preservation of the lot with recommended restoration plans and new amenities.

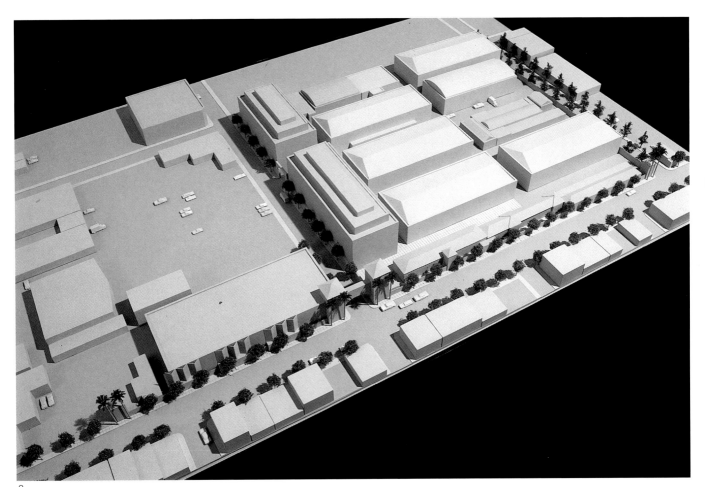

3

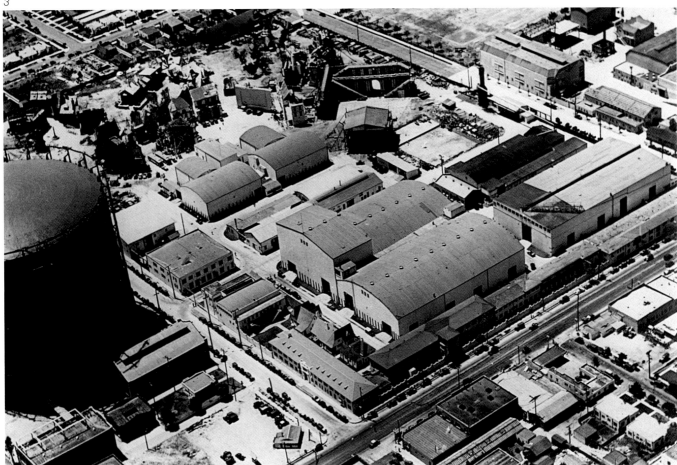

4

SOKA UNIVERSITY OF AMERICA MASTER PLAN

Aliso Viejo, California, 1996

1

204 Situated on 103 acres of steeply sloped land in Orange County, the new campus for Soka University of America (SUA) evokes its educational philosophy. The liberal arts college and graduate school seeks to encourage human development through close interpersonal relationships, and to foster global understanding through coursework involving comparative discussions with various international perspectives. Likewise, planning of the site is at once outward and inward looking. Terraces and overlooks provide sweeping vistas of surrounding canyons and parkland, offering places to reflect and gain perspective. Simultaneously, its self-contained hilltop environment, enclosed by a ring road and embellished with a patchwork of plazas and green spaces, provides an intimate cloister.

Planning for the four-year campus is based upon the notion of an academic village. Mediterranean-style buildings with contemporary interpretations, terraced into hillsides, are intersected by ramps, steps, trails, gardens, and courtyards. The complex emphasizes the connection between people and their environment, both natural and man-made. Electronic connections exist as well, with network capabilities inside all buildings and outside in gathering places, allowing learning and connectivity to the global environment to occur anywhere and everywhere on campus.

Development is occurring in phases, beginning with the campus core, which includes more than 500,000 square feet of facilities. Rather than a campus "waiting to happen," a physical environment that fully supports academic and social objectives will surround SUA's first students. With the judicious placement of residence halls, the library, faculty offices/classroom buildings, University Center, and the recreation center and natatorium, the campus is planned to feel complete, even during initial stages.

When fully built, SUA will serve as many as 2500 students. It will include additional classrooms, laboratories, administrative offices, and residence halls as well as a fine and performing arts center.

Facilities are concentrated to encourage student and faculty dialogue. Passages between buildings contain small plazas, terraces, gardens, and colonnades. These are complemented by larger outdoor spaces ranging from informal campus greens to manicured lawns, orchards, hillsides, and lakeside esplanades. Opportunities for social interaction, relaxation, recreation, and contemplation are plentiful.

The Japanese word "soka" means "to create value." As envisioned by its founder, noted educator and philosopher Daisaku Ikeda, the university will foster individuals who seek to achieve wisdom and exemplary character as they learn the value of service to others and to the natural world around them. The new SUA campus offers an idyllic setting in which to exercise these principles. An environment that preserves the natural beauty of the terrain, an architecture that signifies permanence and seriousness of purpose, and a physical setting that demonstrates social responsibility and stewardship of the land become a training ground for new generations of global citizens.

1. Site model of fully developed master plan
2. Open space/pedestrian circulation plan
3. Rendering of campus

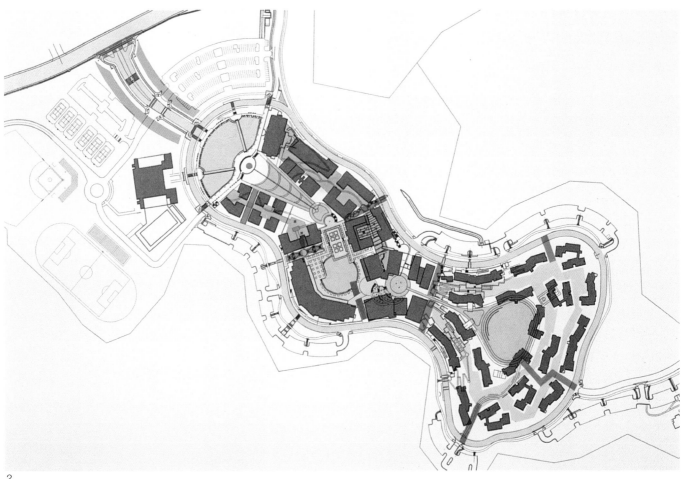

2

3

OLYMPIC VILLAGE 2008 MASTER PLAN

New York, New York, 1996

206 In preparation of submitting a formal bid for New York City to host the 2008 summer Olympics, NYC 2008, a nonprofit Olympic steering committee, asked HHPA to develop plans for an Olympic Village in Manhattan. Two sites were selected along the Hudson River. The "ground rules" for planning were that each village had to embrace Olympic traditions, provide a secure yet welcoming environment, accommodate more than 900,000 square feet of programmed space, and effectively convert after the Olympics into self-contained residential communities.

Piers now occupy both locations. The lower Manhattan site, "Olympic Isles," is immediately north of Battery Park City; the "42nd-Street Olympic Village Piers" is located in midtown. Each site is planned to house 420,000 square feet of indoor training facilities, 5000 residential units, the National Olympic Committee headquarters, a poly-clinic, restaurants, entertainment and dining facilities for the athletes, workshops, changing areas, and Village Square — a large public plaza and the site for Olympic ceremonies. Post-Olympic conversion reuses these facilities and spaces for schools, recreation, public plazas, and a variety of retail, enter-tainment, and dining services indispensable to a vibrant residential community.

Though the two sites accommodate similar activities, their sensitivity to context results in unique design solutions. Planning for Olympic Isles expands both the gridlike street pattern of nearby Tribeca and the open-space pedestrian concepts of Battery Park City. Its village is conceived as a self-contained island with secured bridges providing athletes controlled access and a private riverfront promenade. A walk through its park offers a vista of Liberty Park and the Statue of Liberty, a reminder of Manhattan's historic role in welcoming people from all lands. Athletes live within a neighborhood setting of mid-rise buildings surrounding open courtyards.

At the games' conclusion, security points are removed and residential blocks are woven back into the fabric of the city. Training facilities are converted to schools, and Village Square becomes a public gathering space. The established promenades along the riverfront extend Battery Park City to

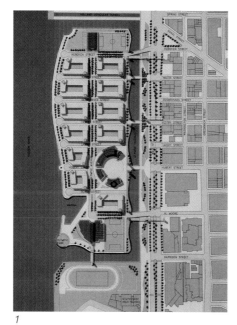

1

Canal Street, while pedestrian bridges connect the island to nearby educational institutions, giving them access to shared outdoor recreational facilities.

By contrast, the 42nd-Street Olympic Village Piers offers athletes accommodations in four luxury high-rises and an international zone in which to relax, shop, and socialize. A series of stepped towers rise up in scale from the adjacent Clinton neighborhood to full height at river's edge. Their vertical forms echo waterfront piers. Rooftop gardens provide Olympians with private outdoor space and spectacular waterfront and skyline vistas. Beaconlike fixtures atop each tower are reminiscent of lighthouses that once signaled safe passage for those entering the city.

This site offers visitors an opportunity to experience the best the city has to offer. With splendid views of Manhattan and residences located within walking distance of scores of retail and entertainment amenities, athletes will feel very much a part of the city. Within the village they can enjoy a variety of leisure activities, including movie theaters, game rooms, a library, and worship and meditation areas; shopping, retail, and service facilities; and a logistics center for VIPs and media. These attractions in conjunction with the upscale apartments and pedestrian esplanades are ideal for a

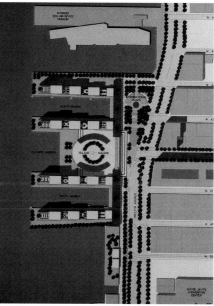

2

transition to a new residential neighborhood in the heart of midtown.

Concepts for an Olympic Village exude the vitality of Manhattan while maintaining security levels necessary to insure the safety of Olympians. Each site captures the spirit of its setting and reflects the city's rich history as host to all creeds and cultures. Each village will thrive well past 2008 as a welcome addition to its community.

---

1. Olympic Isles site plan
2. 42nd-Street Olympic Village Piers site plan
3. Olympic Isles looking north
4. Olympic Isles looking west
5. Aerial view of 42nd-Street Olympic Village Piers
6. Aerial view of Olympic Isles

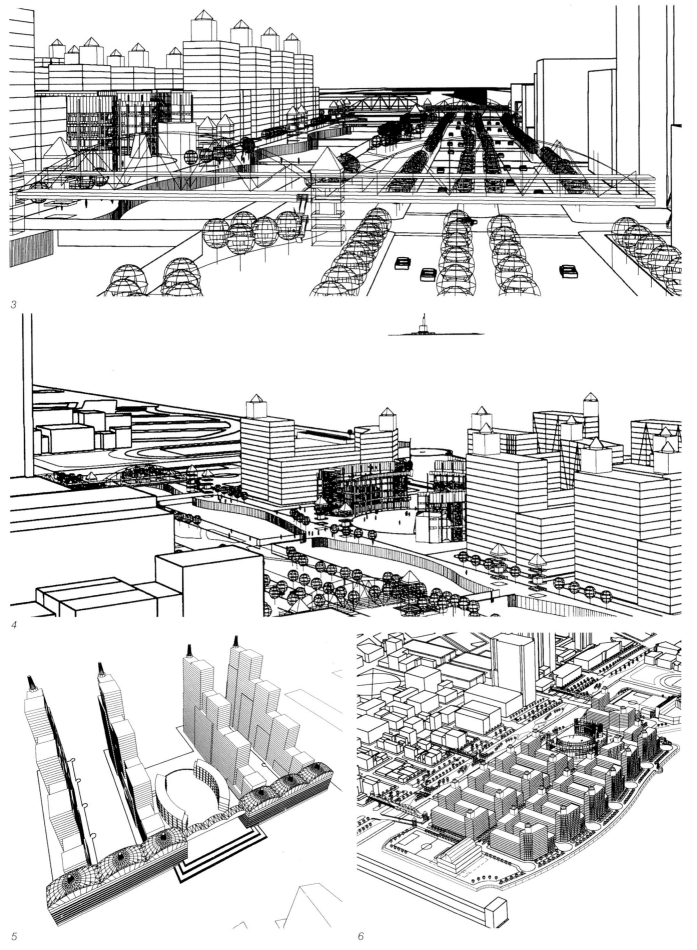

3

4

5

6

FRANCISCAN UNIVERSITY OF STEUBENVILLE MASTER PLAN

Steubenville, Ohio, 1989, 1995, 1998

1. Aerial view of campus
2. Pedestrian circulation plan
3. Master plan
4. Finnegan Field House

208

In 1960 Franciscan University of Steubenville acquired two parcels of farmland on the bluffs overlooking the Ohio River, and began to build its new campus. Much of the landscape's natural beauty had previously been stripped, and buildings were randomly placed on the barren site. When HHPA was commissioned, in 1989, to design the new Finnegan Field House one of the issues in siting the facility was the desire to have it central to campus life and not just a perimeter outpost. The campus lacked a sense of place and did not reflect the spiritual and physical nature of the university.

To establish an identity for the campus and transform its 120 acres into an appropriate setting for study and contemplation, a long-range plan was initiated. HHPA's efforts were premised on the belief that incremental changes in the landscape, pedestrian and vehicular circulation, location of parking, and the sensitive design and placement of new construction could convert a somewhat undistinguished campus into an attractive academic environment.

The plan reinforces and accommodates the university's projected expansion requirements over twenty years and provides a consistent course of development. Considering the cohesive nature of the campus for the first time, it focuses activity in dedicated areas, maximizes views of the river, and establishes orientation points.

Recommendations for placement of new buildings allow for concentration of related activities, reinforcement of pedestrian routes, and creation of courtyard enclosures. A key factor in the plan's success is removal of vehicular traffic from the campus core to a ring road. New landscape features strengthen the pedestrian spine that links academic, student life, and living areas. Pathways through the hilltop's undulating topography encourage contemplation.

Accomplishment of these first initiatives, including construction of several new facilities and outdoor gathering places, promoted the university's sense of community. In 1995 HHPA updated the master plan to site a new chapel, 300 dormitory rooms, a science facility, and athletic fields. Placement of these new

1

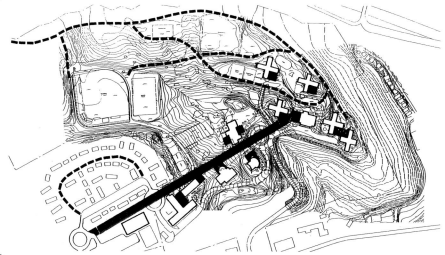

2

buildings and spaces maintains all of the principles of the original plan, yet provides for additional development not previously contemplated. Their locations increase the density in the three campus areas, support visual corridors, and help define the edges of the central campus.

The most recent update, undertaken in 1998, explores new campus housing. Careful siting permits the development of courtyards between buildings and completes the residential precinct envisioned earlier. HHPA also evaluated future sites for a new

guesthouse and outreach facility. Pathways were defined to afford river views and spaces for refuge.

Through careful implementation of the master plan over time, discreet changes have indeed profoundly shaped the campus. New outdoor places for congregation and respite, plantings that direct attention to natural scenic features, and greater concentration of buildings have established an academic environment appropriate to the landscape of the Ohio River valley and to the mission of the institution.

3

4

SALT LAKE CITY CULTURAL PLAN

Salt Lake City, Utah, 1999

210

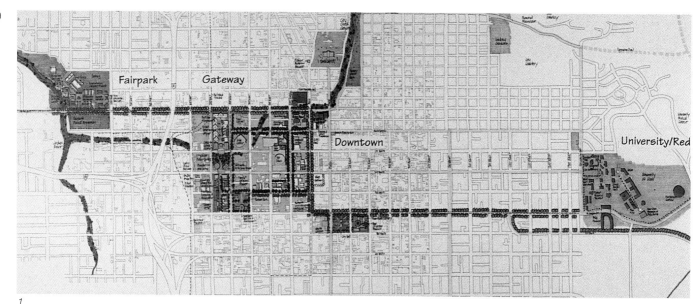

Fairpark   Gateway

Downtown

University/Red

1

Salt Lake City, which has thirty-one major performance and exhibition venues, more than eight million visitors a year, and the world at its door for the 2002 Winter Olympics, would like further to strengthen its position as a recognized center for cultural activities. At the city Redevelopment Agency's request, HHPA is preparing a comprehensive strategic plan that supports the expansion goals of arts institutions in coordination with proposed transportation improvements. The goal is to establish the city as an economically, ethnically, and artistically diverse center of commercial and cultural activity for the region.

The study team met with directors of arts organizations, civic leaders, and community representatives to gain an understanding of existing programs, cultural offerings, and facilities within the region, including those at the University of Utah. In addition to addressing the potential for physical improvements and new construction, opportunities were explored for "cross fertilization" through joint facilities, satellite offerings, coordinated programming, and outreach efforts.

Four cultural campuses stretching from Utah State Fairpark to the Red Butte Garden were identified as hubs of activity. Their location along the city's extensive bicycle-path system and light-rail line will

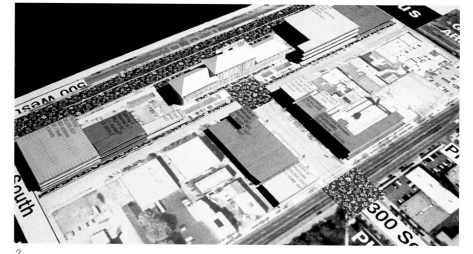

2

maximize investments in transportation. The plan proposes to link these campuses visually through a well-defined way-finding system of landscape, lighting, banners, and streetscape amenities. New arts facilities and programs, pedestrian connections, and mixed-use developments will create synergy between religious, education, research, and cultural institutions. Recommendations for the reuse of historic structures and existing properties are integral elements of the overall vision. One component of the project, a concept design for a new multicultural center, seeks to redevelop a site within 680 acres of abandoned railway yards.

As many American cities have discovered, the presence of performing and visual arts institutions is a powerful force in the revitalization of downtown neighborhoods. Tourism and entertainment are also major contributors to a region's economic development. The strategic plan for Salt Lake City coalesces cultural institutions and is an effective fundraising tool for realizing future growth. By joining plans for expansion with larger civic initiatives, Salt Lake City will be able to offer citizens and visitors alike a host of attractions in cohesive and easily accessible zones of activity.

3

4

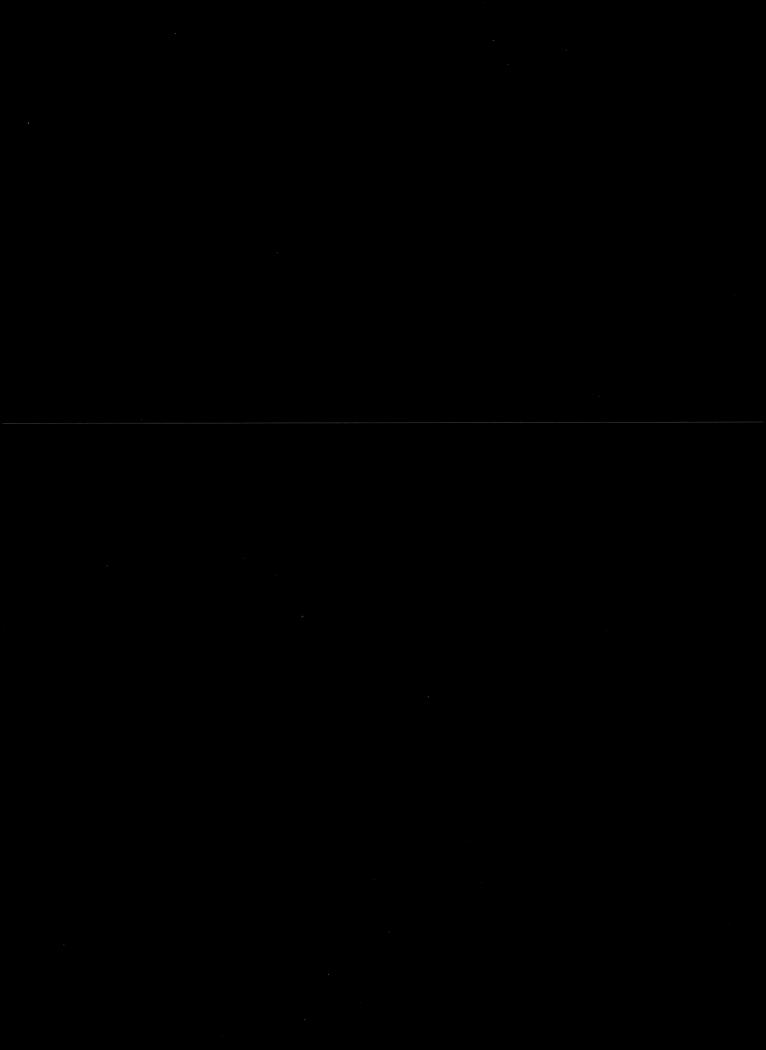

APPENDICES

Academy of American Poets
New York, New York, 1992
New construction
Academy of American Poets, Inc.

American Industrial Partners Offices
New York, New York, 1993 and 1995
New construction
American Industrial Partners

New York Botanical Garden Janet and Arthur Ross Lecture Hall
Bronx, New York, 1993
Renovation
New York Botanical Garden

University of California, San Diego Bio-Medical Library
La Jolla, California, 1993 Design
Renovation and new construction
University of California, San Diego

University of Southern California Music School and Concert Hall
Los Angeles, California, 1994 Design
New construction
University of Southern California

Union College, Yulman Theater
Schenectady, New York, 1995
New construction
Union College

Capriccio Restaurant
Cooperstown, New York, 1996 Design
New Construction
Glimmerglass Opera Theater

University of Oklahoma Center for Law and International Studies
Norman, Oklahoma, 1996 Design
Renovation and new construction
University of Oklahoma

Wilma Theater
Philadelphia, Pennsylvania, 1996
New construction
Wilma Theater

Glimmerglass Administration Building
Cooperstown, New York, 1997
New construction
Glimmerglass Opera Theater

Glimmerglass Pavilion
Cooperstown, New York, 1997
New construction
Glimmerglass Opera Theater

Paramount Building Spectacular Sign
New York, New York, 1997
Signage
ArtKraft Strauss Sign Corporation

Village Eateries
New York, New York Casino Hotel,
Las Vegas, Nevada, 1997
New construction
Ark Restaurants

Alfred University International Museum of Ceramic Art
Alfred, New York, 1998 Design
New construction
Alfred University

Carnegie Observatory Library
Pasadena, California, 1998
Renovation
Institute of the Carnegie Observatories

Clemson University Hendrix Student Center
Clemson, South Carolina, 1998
New construction
Clemson University

Compass Rose Restaurant
Singapore, 1998 Design
New construction
Raffles Corporation

Long Wharf Theatre
New Haven, Connecticut, 1998
Renovation
Long Wharf Theatre

Minnesota Orchestra Hall
Minneapolis, Minnesota, 1998
Renovation
Minnesota Orchestral Association

New Harbor Offices
New York, New York, 1998
New construction
New Harbor Incorporated

New York School of Interior Design
New York, New York, 1998
Renovation and new construction
New York School of Interior Design

21 West Street
New York, New York, 1998
Renovation
Rose Associates, Inc.

Vivian Beaumont and Mitzi Newhouse Theaters
New York, New York, 1998
Renovation and new construction
Lincoln Center Theater

Battery Park City Residential Site 12
New York, New York, In Progress
New construction
Opus Three Limited and The Brodsky
Organization

Battery Park City Residential Site 13
New York, New York, In Progress
New construction
DeMatteis Organization

**California State University, Fullerton
Fine and Performing Arts Center**
Fullerton, California, In Progress
New construction
California State University, Fullerton

**California State University, Northridge
Administration Building**
Northridge, California, In Progress
New construction
California State University, Northridge

California Western School of Law
San Diego, California, In Progress
New construction
California Western School of Law

Calvary Church of Pacific Palisades
Pacific Palisades, California, In Progress
New construction
Calvary Church of Pacific Palisades

**Central Connecticut State University
Student Center**
New Britain, Connecticut, In Progress
Renovation and new construction
Central Connecticut State University

Central Synagogue
New York, New York, In Progress
Restoration
Central Synagogue

**Chatham-Effingham-Liberty
Regional Library**
Savannah, Georgia, In Progress
Renovation and new construction
Chatham-Effingham-Liberty Regional Library

Colburn Conservatory
Los Angeles, California, In Progress
New construction
Colburn School for Performing Arts

Colgate University Student Activity Centers
Hamilton, New York, In Progress
Renovation and new construction
Colgate University

Coronado Public Library
Coronado, California, In Progress
Renovation and new construction
Coronado Public Library

Court Street Development
Brooklyn, New York, In Progress
New construction
Forest City Ratner

Daniel Boone Regional Library
Columbia, Missouri, In Progress
Renovation and new construction
Columbia Public Library

Grand Rapids Public Library
Grand Rapids, Michigan, In Progress
Renovation and new construction
Grand Rapids Public Library

Griffith Observatory
Los Angeles, California, In Progress
Renovation and new construction
City of Los Angeles

Herald and Greeley Squares
New York, New York, In Progress
New construction
The 34th Street Partnership

Hippodrome Performing Arts Center
Baltimore, Maryland, In Progress
Renovation and new construction
Maryland Stadium Authority

Hyperion Theater
Anaheim, California, In Progress
New construction
Confidential

Musical Theatre Works
New York, New York, In Progress
Renovation
Musical Theatre Works, Inc.

New Offices
Connecticut, In Progress
New construction
Confidential

New York City Public Schools
Brooklyn, New York, In Progress
Renovation and new construction
New York City School Construction Authority

**Northwestern University Norris
University Center**
Evanston, Illinois, In Progress
Renovation and new construction
Northwestern University

Penn Station Redevelopment
New York, New York, In Progress
Renovation and reuse
Penn Station Redevelopment Corporation

Pima County Community College
Tucson, Arizona, In Progress
Renovation and new construction
Pima County Community College

Princeton University McCarter Theatre
Princeton, New Jersey, In Progress
New construction and renovation
Princeton University

P. S. 69
Brooklyn, New York, In Progress
New construction
New York City School Construction Authority

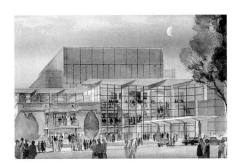

RiverCenter for the Performing Arts Center
Columbus, Georgia, In Progress
New construction
Columbus State University/
Downtown Development Authority

Santa Monica Main Library
Santa Monica, California, In Progress
Renovation and new construction
City of Santa Monica

770 Broadway
New York, New York, In Progress
Renovation
Mendik Realty Company, Inc.

216 **Solow Restaurant**
New York, New York, In Progress
New construction
Solow Development Corporation

Texas Tech University, University Center
Lubbock, Texas, In Progress
New Construction
Texas Tech University

University of Miami Music School
Coral Gables, Florida, In Progress
New construction
University of Miami

University of Miami Richter Library
Coral Gables, Florida, In Progress
Renovation and new construction
University of Miami

Seattle King Street Station
Seattle, Washington, In Progress
Renovation
Washington State Department of Transportation

**University of Notre Dame Marie P.
DeBartolo Center for the Performing Arts**
Notre Dame, Indiana, In Progress
New construction
University of Notre Dame

University of Oklahoma Law Library
Norman, Oklahoma, In Progress
New construction
University of Oklahoma

University of the South Dining Hall
Sewanee, Tennessee, In Progress
New construction
University of the South

Amon Carter Museum
Fort Worth, Texas, 1992
Long Range Plan
Amon Carter Museum

Santa Clarita Ranch
Los Angeles County, California, 1993
Master Plan
Warner Bros.

**University of Kentucky Clifton Circle
Academic Core**
Lexington, Kentucky, 1993
Master Plan
University of Kentucky

Chatham Hall
Chatham, Virginia, 1994
Master Plan
Chatham Hall

**Vail Valley Performance
and Conference Center**
Vail, Colorado, 1994
Feasibility Study
Town of Vail

California State University, Ventura
Ventura, California, 1995
Master Plan
California State University

Cornell University Bailey Hall
Ithaca, New York, 1995
Improvements Study
Cornell University

National Actors' Theatre
New York, New York, 1995
Feasibility Study
National Actors' Theatre

Ormond Beach
Oxnard, California, 1995
Specific Development Plan
City of Oxnard

**University of Minnesota
Northrup Auditorium**
Minneapolis, Minnesota, 1995
Improvements Study
University of Minnesota

Fort Collins Performing Arts Center
Fort Collins, Colorado, 1996
Feasibility Study
Colorado State University/City of Fort Collins

Idylease Inn & Resort
Newfoundland, New Jersey, 1996
Master Plan
Z-Boys, Inc.

New Haven Cultural Arts
New Haven, Connecticut, 1996
District Plan
City of New Haven

San Francisco Emporium
San Francisco, California, 1997
Project
Forest City Ratner

Boston Central Library: Central Library
Boston, Massachusetts, 1998
Master Plan
City of Boston

California State University, Monterey Bay Festival Center
Monterey Bay, California, 1998
Feasibility Study
California State University

California State University, Channel Islands
Camarillo, California, 1998
Master Plan
California State University

Center for Culture and Creativity
Salt Lake City, Utah, 1998
Feasibility Study
Utah Cultural Campus Project

Delaware Art Museum
Wilmington, Delaware, 1998
Strategic Building and Site Development Plan
Delaware Art Museum

Lansing Performing Arts Center
Lansing, Michigan, 1998
Feasibility Study
City of Lansing

Middle Country Public Library
Centereach and Selden, New York, 1998
Planning Study for Renovation and Expansion
Middle Country Public Library

New Jersey Railroad and Transportation Heritage Center
New Jersey, 1998
Feasibility Study and Master Plan
New Jersey Railroad and Transportation
Heritage Center Commission

New York City School Construction Authority Library Standards
New York City, New York, 1998
Standards
New York City School Construction Authority

New York Stock Exchange
New York, New York, 1998
Planning Study for renovation and expansion
New York Stock Exchange, Inc.

Oklahoma History Center
Oklahoma City, Oklahoma, 1998
Feasibility Study
Oklahoma Historical Society

Omaha Symphony
Omaha, Nebraska, 1998
Feasibility Study
Omaha Symphony Association

Peabody Institute
Baltimore, Maryland, 1998
Master Plan
Johns Hopkins University

San Diego Civic Theater
San Diego, California, 1998
Improvements Study
San Diego Convention Center Corporation

Shubert Organization 499-Seat Theater at Theater Row
New York, New York, 1998
Feasibility Study
Shubert Organization

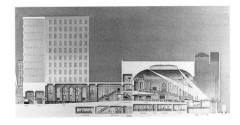

Tennessee Theater
Knoxville, Tennessee, 1998
Feasibility Study
Tennessee Theater

University of New Mexico Enchanted Skies Park
Horace Mesa, New Mexico, 1998
Master Plan
University of New Mexico

Arena Stage
Washington, D.C., In Progress
Planning Study for Renovation and Expansion
Arena Stage

Long Wharf Theatre
New Haven, Connecticut, In Progress
Programming and Cost and Site Analyses
Long Wharf Theatre

New Haven Arts and Entertainment Study
New Haven, Connecticut, In Progress
Master Plan
Arts Council of Greater New Haven

Pima County Community College
Tucson, Arizona, In Progress
Master Plan
Pima County Community College

Shubert Organization Theater at Rock West
New York, New York, In Progress
Feasibility Study
Shubert Organization

Shubert Organization
New York, New York, In Progress
ADA Study
Shubert Organization

St. Clement's Episcopal Church
New York, New York, In Progress
Master Plan
St. Clement's Episcopal Church

SUNY Purchase Music Pavilion
Purchase, New York, In Progress
Feasibility Study
Purchase College

University of Notre Dame Washington and Crowley Halls
Notre Dame, Indiana, In Progress
Feasibility Study for Renovation
University of Notre Dame

Westside Interfaith Center
New York, New York, In Progress
Project
Church of St. Paul and St. Andrew
United Methodist

Competitions

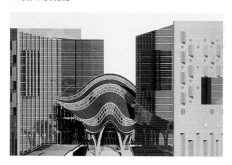

AWARDS SINCE 1992

Firm Awards
Architectural Digest Top 100 Interior Designers and Architects,1995

Interior Design Hall of Fame, Interior Design Magazine, 1992

42nd Street Preservation and Restoration
Metropolitan Historic Structures Association/ National Arts Club: Preservation Award, 1998

Bryant Park and Fifth Avenue Terrace of the New York Public Library
Environmental Design Association: EDRA/Places Award for Design, 1998

Urban Land Institute: Award for Excellence, 1996

AIA: Honor Award for Urban Design, 1994

American Society of Landscape Architects: Design Merit Award, 1994

Cleveland Public Library
The Ceramic Tile Promotion Fund of Greater New York & New Jersey: Celebration of Tile Architectural Project Award, 1998

Greater Cleveland Growth Association: 19th Annual Downtown Recognition Award, 1998

Tile Promotion Board Spectrum International Awards: Grand Award, 1997

The Builders Exchange: 40th Annual Craftsmanship Award, 1997

Northern Ohio Live Magazine: Award of Achievement for Architecture, 1997

Multnomah County Central Library
American Public Works Association: Public Works Project of the Year, 1998

Livable Oregon: Governor's Livability Award, 1998

New Amsterdam Theatre
Victorian Society in America: Award for Preservation Achievement, Interior Restoration, 1998

United States Institute for Theatre Technology: Award, 1998

AIA: Award for Interiors, 1998

AIA New York Chapter: Interior Architecture Award Citation, 1998

The New York Section Illuminating Engineering Society: Lumen Citation, 1998

The Municipal Art Society of New York and Williams Real Estate: New York Preservation Award, 1997

New York State Office of Parks, Recreation and Historic Preservation: New York State Historic Preservation Award, 1997

National Trust for Historic Preservation: National Preservation Honor Award, 1997

New York State Association of Architects/AIA: Excellence in Design Award, 1997

Salisbury Upper School
New York State Association of Architects/AIA: Award of Merit, 1998

Soka University of America
ASLA and Landscape Architecture Magazine: Planning and Urban Design Merit Award, 1997

Southern California Chapter of the ASLA: Quality of Life Award, 1997

New Victory Theater
AIA: Honor Award for Interiors, 1997

United States Institute for Theatre Technology: Architecture Honor Award, 1997

New York State Association of Architects/AIA: Excellence in Design Award, 1996

Alliance for the Arts: Brendan Gill Prize, 1995

Punahou School, Dillingham Hall
AIA: Honor Award for Interiors, 1997

United States Institute for Theatre Technology: Architecture Merit Award, 1997

Stanford University, Language Corner
California Preservation Foundation: Preservation Design Award for Craftsmanship/Preservation Technology, 1997

Hawaii Theatre Center
New York State Association of Architects/AIA: Excellence in Design Award, 1996

Bowdoin College, David Saul Smith Union
AIA: Honor Award for Interiors, 1996

Buildings Magazine: Modernization Award, 1996

Evo A. DeConcini Federal Building and U.S. Courthouse
General Services Administration: Design Award for Building in Progress, 1996

Los Angeles Public Library: Central Library Rehabilitation and Tom Bradley Wing
American Library Association/AIA: Excellence for Library: Architecture Award, 1995

AIA: Honor Award for Urban Design, 1995

Los Angeles Conservancy: Preservation Award, 1994

Interiors Magazine Honor Award: Restoration of the Year–15th Annual Awards, 1993

BAM Majestic Theatre
United States Institute for Theatre Technology: Architecture Honor Award, 1995

Dance Theatre of Harlem
The Art Commission of New York City: Award for Excellence in Design, 1993

University of Nebraska at Omaha Weber Fine Arts Building
Nebraska Chapter/AIA: Distinguished Accomplishment in Architecture Award, 1993

Nebraska Masonry Institute: Honor Award For Innovative Excellence in Masonry, 1993

Stanford University Memorial Church
Consulting Engineers and Land Surveyors of California: Kenward S. Oliphant Memorial Award for Outstanding Engineering Achievement (Seismic Design), 1993

California Preservation Foundation: Preservation/Stabilization Award, 1992

220

Bottom row left to right: Robert Almodovar, Pamela Loeffelman, Daria Pizzetta, William Murray, Robin Kunz, David Saviola, Nestor Bottino, Jean Marie Gath

Top row left to right: Hugh Hardy, James Brogan, Cleveland Adams, Stewart Jones, Douglas Moss, Stephen Johnson, Sharon Lasoff, Edward Carfagno, Norman Pfeiffer, Jack Martin, Malcolm Holzman

Hugh Hardy, FAIA, Founding Partner: Since founding the firm in 1967, Mr. Hardy has directed projects of every scale and type. In recent years he has orchestrated some of HHPA's most significant cultural projects whose energy have helped enrich and reinvigorate the cities in which they stand. Hardy's commitment to the creation of public gathering spaces has been recognized with such distinguished awards as the AIA Honor Award for Urban Design, the Kitty Carlisle Hart Award, and the Brendan Gill Prize. He also received a presidential appointment to the National Council on the Arts of the National Endowment for the Arts in 1992 and was asked by the GSA to serve as both a member of the jury and as chairman of the Evaluation Board of the World War II Memorial in Washington, D.C.

Malcolm Holzman, FAIA, Founding Partner: In thirty-two years of practice Mr. Holzman has designed a wide range of building types that have been constructed in more than twenty-five states. His innovative vision in analyzing programs, generating building plans, and incorporating art has resulted in highly individual and distinctive projects. He was appointed Saarinen Visiting Professor of Architectural Design at Yale University in 1976. He has subsequently held similar positions at the following schools of architecture: University of Wisconsin, Lawrence Technical University, Ball State University, Rensselaer Polytechnic Institute, and the University of Texas. He is recognized internationally for his innovative and economic utilization of stone and the application of prefabricated building components. He is the American architectural contributor for *The Art Book,* and a member of the

editorial advisory board of the *Mac Journal* of the Mackintosh School of Architecture.

Norman Pfeiffer, FAIA, Founding Partner: After nineteen years of practice in HHPA's New York office, Mr. Pfeiffer moved to Los Angeles in 1986 to open the West Coast office. Here he has overseen some of the region's most ambitious architectural commissions. Pfeiffer's portfolio is diverse and includes contemporary new construction as well as historic renovations and additions. He is an active participant in the profession—since 1989 he has served on the Architectural Commission of the University of Washington. He is a frequent contributor to discussions on the issues of architecture and urbanism and has been profiled in a number of regional and national magazines including *American Architecture Now.*

Stephen Johnson, AIA, Associate Partner: A member of HHPA since 1981 and Associate Partner of the firm, Mr. Johnson relocated to Los Angeles in 1986 to establish the L.A. office with Norman Pfeiffer. As project director and head of HHPA's Library Group, he has led many of the firm's most complex projects, including the planning and development of more than a dozen library projects worldwide. He is recognized as an expert in historic preservation and directs HHPA's rehabilitation projects in the western United States. He is vice president of the Los Angeles Conservancy as well as a member of the American Library Association, the California Preservation Foundation, the National Trust for Historic Preservation, and the Society of Campus and University Planners.

Robert Almodovar, AIA, Senior Associate: Mr. Almodovar has worked on the firm's most significant civic libraries and academic buildings since joining HHPA in 1986. On sabbatical from HHPA in the 1994–95 academic year, he was a visiting professor at the Clemson University College of Architecture.

Jean Marie Gath, Senior Associate: Director of the Planning and the Educational Programming Group, Ms. Gath oversees the firm's campus, facility, and land-use planning and programming assignments as well as its urban-design and strategic-development efforts. Gath is a Fellow of the Institute for Urban Design and a member of the American Planning Association, the Society for Campus and University Planners, and the Urban Design Advisory Coalition.

Stewart Jones, AIA, Senior Associate: Mr. Jones is codirector of the firm's Performing Arts Group. A recognized expert in the theater industry, he has managed more than eighteen theater projects since joining HHPA's New York office in 1982. Jones has also served as project director for the firm's historic preservation, science center, and commercial projects. He is a member of the United States Institute of Theater Technology, the National Historic Trust, the League of Historic American Theatres, and the Architectural League of New York.

Pamela Loeffelman, AIA, Senior Associate: Since joining HHPA in 1980, Ms. Loeffelman has served as project manager for some of the firm's most highly acclaimed work in the public and academic sectors. As director of the Museum Group, she has orchestrated the successful realization of several visual arts projects. Loeffelman's recent speaking engagements include the 1998 AIA Convention, the 1998 Urban School Conference, and the Association of Campus Unions International 1998 Pre-Conference and 1999 Annual Conference.

Jack Martin, AIA, Senior Associate: Mr. Martin has directed the design and construction of educational buildings, theaters, and office facilities since joining HHPA in 1980. His recent efforts include the development of urban retail and entertainment complexes. Martin's professional activities include lecturing on systems integration at the 1998 National AIA conference and membership on the AIA Zoning Committee.

William Murray, AIA, Senior Associate: Mr. Murray is codirector of the firm's Performing Arts Group. His experience includes feasibility studies, new construction, and renovation of cultural centers. Since joining HHPA's Los Angeles office in 1991, Murray has developed visual arts, educational, commercial, and civic projects. He is a member of the United States Institute of Theater Technology and the International Association of Assembly Managers.

Cleveland Adams, AIA, Associate: Mr. Adams joined HHPA in 1986 and spent several years engaged in the firm's academic projects before leaving to start his own practice. In 1994 he rejoined the firm and has since been involved in education projects at all levels. Adams specializes in the design of K–12 educational facilities and leads the firm's efforts in public school design. He is a member of the Society of College and University Planners and the AIA Committee on Education.

Caroline Bertrand, Associate: Ms. Bertrand is the design director of the firm's interiors department. Since joining HHPA in 1991, she has led design efforts for numerous projects including new and historic performing arts facilities, restaurants, student centers, and museums. Bertrand serves on the advisory board for the International Contemporary Furniture Fair.

Nestor Bottino, AIA, Associate: Mr. Bottino has served as project architect and manager on a broad range of projects since joining HHPA in 1987. Recently he has concentrated on facilities for the performing and visual arts in the academic and civic sectors. Bottino was a featured speaker on materials use and customization at the 1998 AIA Convention and currently serves as a visiting professor at the University of Texas School of Architecture.

James R. Brogan, AIA, Associate: Mr. Brogan joined HHPA in 1990 and became the firm's director of Information Technology in 1996. He oversees all corporate-wide technology issues. He is chair of the AIA NY Computer Applications Committee and a member of the AIA Computer Aided Practice Advisory Board. Since 1991, he has served as an instructor in the Architecture and Environmental Design Department of Parsons School of Design.

Edward L. Carfagno, AIA, Associate: Mr. Carfagno joined HHPA in 1996 as director of one of the firm's largest commissions, overseeing the design, production, and construction of a new university campus. Carfagno's experience includes hospitality, transportation, commercial office, justice, and public sector projects as well as programming and master planning efforts.

Robin Kunz, Associate: Throughout her seventeen years with HHPA, Ms. Kunz has overseen the interior design and planning on many of HHPA's award-winning public, cultural and academic projects. In 1994 she moved west to establish and direct the interiors department for the Los Angeles office's national and international projects.

Sharon K. Lasoff, Associate: Ms. Lasoff has ten years of experience in marketing and public relations for architectural firms and has been with HHPA since 1993. She is member of numerous professional organizations, including the American Library Association, the American Association of Museums, the Association of Science and Technology Centers, the Urban Land Institute, and the Society for College and University Planning.

Douglas Moss, AIA, Associate: For the past eight years at HHPA, Mr. Moss has been actively involved in the administration and staffing of the office and has worked on a variety of projects, from performing-arts facilities to museums, restaurants, and student centers. Moss has lectured at several universities as well as participated in architectural accreditation visits for national schools of architecture. He serves on both the AIA Professional Practice Committee and the AIA Education Committee.

Daria Pizzetta, Associate: In 1992 Ms. Pizzetta joined HHPA and two years later became administrative director of its interiors department in New York. She has developed nine library projects in the past six years, integrating new technologies and public amenities into sophisticated library spaces. Pizzetta chairs the AIA/New York State Chapter Interiors Committee and is a member of the American Library Association and the Library Administration and Management Association.

David Saviola, AIA, Associate: Mr. Saviola joined HHPA in 1995 and manages the design, production, and construction of facilities for the arts and education on the West Coast. Recent projects involve the incorporation of flexible and multiple-use building programs for public, private, and community uses.

COLLABORATORS
SINCE 1992

222   *HHPA Office:*
      LA left and NYC right

Partners
Hugh Hardy
Malcolm Holzman
Norman Pfeiffer

Associate Partner
Stephen Johnson

Senior Associates
Robert Almodovar
Jean Marie Gath
Stewart Jones
Pamela Loeffelman
Jack Martin
William Murray

Associates
Cleveland Adams
Caroline Bertrand
Nestor Bottino
James R. Brogan
Edward L. Carfagno
David Hart
Robin Kunz
Sharon K. Lasoff
Douglas Moss
Daria Pizzetta
David Saviola

Design and Production Staff
Yasin Abdullah
David Andrini
Gregory Baker
Steve Benesh

Kate Bowman
Jason Briscoe
Ryan Bussard
Bradford Carpenter
Jason Chang

Yoonsung Cho
Sandra Chow
Carolyn Comer Gmelich
Michael Connolly
Serge Demerjian
Premchand Encarnacion
Mahasti Fakourbayat
Foaad Farah
Jeffrey Fineman
John Fontillas
Nina Freedman
Doug Freeman
Angel Gabriel
Octavian Geliman
Massoud Ghassem
Christopher C. Hahn
Danielle Halter
Andrei Harwell
Carlos Hernandez
Gabriel Hernandez
Kyoko Hibino
Marina Himanen
Maria Horta
Thomas M. Jasmin
Matthew M. Jogan
Scott-Alan Joyce
Chris Kaiser
Carl Karas
Lee Karasick
Theresa Kim
Thomas H. Kim
Stephanie Kingsnorth
Raja Krishnan
Eddie Kung
Jason Kuperman
Juhee Lee-Hartford
Jyh-Ling Lee
Stephen Lee
George Leong
Edward S. Levin

Jeeyoon Lim
Ching-Wen Lin
G. Taylor Louden
Geoffrey Lynch
Steven Maisano
Frank Maldonado
John McNulty
Marcelo C. Méndez
Tom Miera
Juan Minaya
Jacob Morrison
Joseph Mullins
Paul Murphey
Samer Nasser
Mindy No
Ryoko Okada
Arturo Padilla
Karan Paibullert
Douglas Pearl
Heather Perry-Melish
Anthony Poon
Carey Press
Sarah Raines
Gilbert Rocca
Alessandro Sanavio
Sobia Sayeda
Maya Schali
Jonathan Schloss
Melissa Schrock
Sacha Schwarzkopf
Jill Sicinski
Hyungsup Sim
Jim Simmons
Steven Stainbrook
Jennifer Strollo
Samantha Sullivan
Damon Surfas
Michael Sy
Barry Talley
Phillip R. Templeton

Daynard Tullis
Cecilia Valino
Danny Wang
Wei Wang
Patrick Weaver
Winslow Wu
David Zaccheo

Administrative Staff
Jennifer Clark Basso
Michelle Basinger
Lynn E. Bowe
Heather Byron-Cox
Benjamin Chan
Stephen C. Epstein
Damon Hill
Michael Honigstein
Arthur P. Kipel
Shue Fee Liu
Donna Long
Guadalupe G. Lara
Heidi Lyons
Rima Mardirosian
Jessica McCormack
Merton Middleton
Tomofumi Nakanishi
Susan Packard
Timothy Reedy
Gail Testagrossa
Madge Thomas
Tom Vollaro
Debra Waters

**Design and Production Staff
Since 1992**
Juan Abraham
John F. Adamek
Richard Alderiso
Elizabeth Andrin
Paul Appleby

Elizabeth Arko
Hector Arreola
Christopher Bach
Joseph Bahan
J. Shane Baker
Scott Bakos
Daniel Barrenechea
Kin Bassett
Daniel Benjamin
Lourdes Bernard
Paul Boghossian
Beatriz Borquez
Orest Boszko
Manuel Bouza
Sheelagh Brady Saligman
Stuart Brummett
Brent Capron
Sophia Cha
March Chadwick
Vartan Chalikian
Vivian Chan
Hakee Chang
Natalie Cheng
Nicholas Chin
Byung Kook Cho
Macruhi Cialichian
Sally Copeland
Rodrigo Cordero
Roy Cordero
John Crellin
Bernice Davis
Jasmine Davy
Mark DeMarta
Amy C. De Riszner
Nathalie Douge
Kenneth Drucker
James Eddy
Adam Feldman
Rebecca Fenno
David Flynn

John Frost
Michael Gawron
Thomas Gilman
Tina Go
Jacob Goldman
Victor Gong
Kristin Gossman
Robert Gross
Eric Hammerlund
Elizabeth Harrison Kubany
David Herrera
Cathy Hillman
Meg Hironaka
Alicia Hrabia
Eric Hurst
David Johnson
Peter Johnston
Achyut Kantawala
Anne Katata
Louis Kaufman
Jenn Kawakami
Philip Klinkon
Mark Kim
Robert Larlee
Betsey Lau
William Leeds
Elizabeth Leong
Michele Levy
Joo Keong Lim
Camille Loftus
Joyce Louie
Raoul Lowenberg
Frankie Mackay
Elizabeth Martin
Todd Martin
Christopher Mazzier
Samara McCartney
Wendy McGlamery
Sophia McLane
Brian McWatters

Manuel Mergal
Kaori Mikagi
Catherine Minervini
Jennifer Mowery
John Mueller
William Mulvey
John V. E. Murphey
Slawek Nadowski
George Nakatani (in memoriam)
Jefferson Neaves
Kristopher Nikolich
Thomas Nohr
Alex Nussbaumer
Peter Ogman
Setrak K. Ohannessian
Eugene Ong
Kari Overvik
Hannah Pang
John Poelker
Susan Pon
Aron Portnoy
Damon Pressman
Andrew Reeder
Alan Robinson
Victor Rodriguez
Zulma Rodriguez-Ramos
Allison Roede
Duke Sakiyabu
Cynthia Salah
Gilbert Sanchez
Paolo SantíAbrogio
Christoph Schabacker
David Senninger
Guobo Shao
Frank Shih
Karen Singh
Kala Somvanshi
Vera Stevanovic-Hetchel
Douglas Stebbins
Susan Stein

Senzeni Steingruber
Vera Stevanovic-Hetcel
Silvina Suarez
Juliet Taff
George Takoudes
David Tepper
Simon Thakordeen
George Thun
Lynne Thurmond-Brandt
Lucy Timbers
Peiheng Tsai
Esther Tse
Stephen Vetter
Amelia Wagenbach
Kristina Walker
Sherry Wang
Ann Webster
Heather Weiss
David West
Drew Wilson
Frank Wong
Steven Wood
James Woolum
Charlotte Worthy
Peter Wowkowych
Hsin-Yi Wu
Mai Wu
Zhiling Yu
Michael Yung
Bryan Zelnik

PHOTOGRAPHY CREDITS

224   All photos in this book are by Hardy Holzman Pfeiffer Associates except those listed below. Page numbers are followed by figure numbers in parentheses.

Peter Aaron/© ESTO Photographics: 33, 34 (2), 35

© Russell Abraham: 164 (3), 165

© The Air Photo Archives, Department of Geography, UCLA : 201 (4)

Courtesy of the BAM Archives: 134 (1)

© Craig Blackmon: 153 (4, 5), 7

© Erik Borg: 17 (32), 26 (2), 31* (12)

Courtesy of Bowdoin College: 72 (7)

© Jack Brennan: 174 (2)

© Brian Vanden Brink: 70 (1, 2), 71, 72 (5, 6), 73

© Anne Brown: 177 (5)

Ken Burris/© Middlebury College: 27 (3)

© F. Charles: 22 (2)

© Whitney Cox: 120 (6, 9), 137–139

© Used by permission from Disney Enterprises, Inc.: 14 (19), 16 (28), 100 (1), 119 (Disney characters © Disney Enterprises, Inc.),120 (7, 8), 121–123

© Foaad Farah: 14 (22), 15 (24, 27), 17 (31), 46 (1), 47, 48 (4, 5), 50–52, 53 (15, 17), 106 (1, 3), 107–109, 131, 132 (2), 133, 146 (1), 147–151, 166, 167 (7), 184, 186, 187 (2, 3), 193, 194 (1), 195, 200, 201 (3), 208, 215, 218, 222

Courtesy of Franciscan University of Steubenville: 206 (1)

© David Franzen: 66 (1), 68–69, 102 (3), 103–105, 124 (1), 125–127, 152, 153 (6), 154 (7), 155–156

© Blake Gardner: 29 (9)

© Evelyn Hofer: 78 (2), 79 (3), 83

© Timothy Hursley: 85 (2)

© Jennie Jones: 142 (6)

© Elliott Kaufman: 14 (20, 23), 16 (29), 17 (30), 62 (1), 63, 64 (5), 65, 75–77, 78 (1), 80 (4,5), 81–82, 134 (2), 135, 214

Courtesy of The Hawaii Theatre Center: 102 (2)

© Tom Kessler: 13 (17), 36 (1), 37–39, 40 (8, 9, 10, 11, 12), 41, 58–59, 60 (4, 5), 61, 85 (3), 86 (4, 5), 87–91, 93, 94 (2, 3), 95–99, 219

© Christopher Little: 13 (16), 111–115

© Christopher Lovi: 23, 25, 43, 44 (3, 4, 5), 56 (5), 101 (3, 4), 180 (1), 182 (1), 183 (3), 196 (1), 214, 217, 223, 219

© Christopher Lovi and Foaad Farah: 220

© Norman McGrath: 10 (4, 5), 12 (11, 13, 14), 27 (1), 28, 29 (8), 30

© Michael Moran: 158 (1), 159 (3), 161–163, 178 (1), 179 (4)

© James R. Morse: 11 (10), 62 (2, 3), 64 (6)

© Grant Mudford: 8 (1)

© Museum of the City of New York: 118 (1)

© Peter Paige: 57 (6)

Courtesy of Radio City Music Hall Archives: 177 (3, 4, 6)

© Cervin Robinson: 12 (15), 13 (18), 15 (25), 116 (1), 117 (3), 128 (1, 2), 129, 140 (1), 141, 142 (5, 7, 8), 143–145, 190 (1), 219

© J. Brough Schamp: 183 (4, 5)

© Stanford News Service: 164 (2)

© Tim Street-Porter: 11 (9), 53 (16)

© Addison Thompson: 74 (1)

© Jay Venezia: 49 (7)
© Paul Warchol: 11 (8), 15 (26), 21, 24, 54 (1), 55, 56 (4)

© Matt Wargo: 214

© Wisconsin Center for Film and Theater Research: 118 (2), 45 (7)

© Isaiah Wyner: 214

Renderings
James Akers: 179 (5, 6)
Gregory A. Berzinsky: 211 (3)
Jeffrey Crussell: 203 (3, 4)
John Duncan: 189 (3, 4)
Lee Dunnette: 175 (3), 218
Al Forster: 185 (2)
Howard Associates: 181 (3, 5, 6)
Dick Howard: 216
David Purceil: 209 (3), 215
Timothy Slattery: 217